WORKBOOK IN DRAFTING FOR ELECTRONICS
Second Edition

LOUIS GARY LAMIT
Instructor—Computer-Aided Drafting and Design
DeAnza College
Cupertino, CA

DENNIS D. WAHLER
Instructor—Electromechanical Drafting and Design
San Jose City College
San Jose, CA

JOHN J. HIGGINS
Freelance Professional Illustrator
Rohnert Park, CA

Merrill, an imprint of
Macmillan Publishing Company
New York

Maxwell Macmillan Canada
Toronto

Maxwell Macmillan International
New York   Oxford   Singapore   Sydney

Cover art/photo: Jook P. Leung
Editor: Stephen Helba
Developmental Editor: Monica Ohlinger
Production Editor: Colleen Brosnan
Art Coordinator: Lorraine Woost
Text Designer: Debra A. Fargo
Cover Designer: Thomas Mack
Production Buyer: Pamela D. Bennett

This book was set in Times Roman by Bi-Comp, Inc. and was printed and bound by
Semline, Inc./Book Press, Inc., Quebecor America Book Group Companies. The cover
was printed by Phoenix Color Corp.

The Publisher offers discounts on this book when ordered in bulk quantities. For more
information, write to:
    Special Sales Department
    Macmillan Publishing Company
    445 Hutchinson Avenue
    Columbus, OH 43235
or call 1-800-228-7854

Macmillan Publishing Company
866 Third Avenue
New York, NY 10022

Macmillan Publishing Company is part of the Maxwell
Communication Group of Companies.

Maxwell Macmillan Canada, Inc.
1200 Eglinton Avenue East, Suite 200
Don Mills, Ontario M3C 3N1

International Standard Book Number: 0-02-367345-1

Printing: 1 2 3 4 5 6 7 8 9   Year: 3 4 5 6 7

MERRILL'S INTERNATIONAL SERIES IN ENGINEERING TECHNOLOGY

INTRODUCTION TO ENGINEERING TECHNOLOGY

Pond, *Introduction to Engineering Technology, 2nd Edition*, 0-02-396031-0

ELECTRONICS TECHNOLOGY

Electronics Reference

Adamson, *The Electronics Dictionary for Technicians*, 0-02-300820-2
Berlin, *The Illustrated Electronics Dictionary*, 0-675-20451-8
Reis, *Becoming an Electronics Technician: Securing Your High-Tech Future*, 0-02-399231-X

DC/AC Circuits

Boylestad, *DC/AC: The Basics*, 0-675-20918-8
Boylestad, *Introductory Circuit Analysis, 6th Edition*, 0-675-21181-6
Ciccarelli, *Circuit Modeling: Exercises and Software, 2nd Edition*, 0-02-322455-X
Floyd, *Electric Circuits Fundamentals, 2nd Edition*, 0-675-21408-4
Floyd, *Electronics Fundamentals: Circuits, Devices, and Applications, 2nd Edition*, 0-675-21310-X
Floyd, *Principles of Electric Circuits, 4th Edition*, 0-02-338531-6
Floyd, *Principles of Electric Circuits: Electron Flow Version, 3rd Edition*, 0-02-338501-4
Keown, *PSpice and Circuit Analysis*, 0-675-22135-8
Monssen, *PSpice with Circuit Analysis*, 0-675-21376-2
Tocci, *Introduction to Electric Circuit Analysis, 2nd Edition*, 0-675-20002-4

Devices and Linear Circuits

Berlin & Getz, *Fundamentals of Operational Amplifiers and Linear Integrated Circuits*, 0-675-21002-X
Berube, *Electronic Devices and Circuits Using MICRO-CAP II*, 0-02-309160-6
Berube, *Electronic Devices and Circuits Using MICRO-CAP III*, 0-02-309151-7
Bogart, *Electronic Devices and Circuits, 3rd Edition*, 0-02-311701-X
Tocci, *Electronic Devices: Conventional Flow Version, 3rd Edition*, 0-675-21150-6
Floyd, *Electronic Devices, 3rd Edition*, 0-675-22170-6
Floyd, *Electronic Devices: Electron Flow Version*, 0-02-338540-5
Floyd, *Fundamentals of Linear Circuits*, 0-02-338481-6
Schwartz, *Survey of Electronics, 3rd Edition*, 0-675-20162-4
Stanley, *Operational Amplifiers with Linear Integrated Circuits, 2nd Edition*, 0-675-20660-X
Tocci & Oliver, *Fundamentals of Electronic Devices, 4th Edition*, 0-675-21259-6

Digital Electronics

Floyd, *Digital Fundamentals, 4th Edition*, 0-675-21217-0
McCalla, *Digital Logic and Computer Design*, 0-675-21170-0
Reis, *Digital Electronics through Project Analysis* 0-675-21141-7
Tocci, *Fundamentals of Pulse and Digital Circuits, 3rd Edition*, 0-675-20033-4

Microprocessor Technology

Antonakos, *The 68000 Microprocessor: Hardware and Software Principles and Applications, 2nd Edition*, 0-02-303603-6
Antonakos, *An Introduction to the Intel Family of Microprocessors: A Hands-On Approach Utilizing the 8088 Microprocessor*, 0-675-22173-0
Brey, *The Advanced Intel Microprocessors*, 0-02-314245-6
Brey, *The Intel Microprocessors: 8086/8088, 80186, 80286, 80386, and 80486: Architecture, Programming, and Interfacing, 2nd Edition*, 0-675-21309-6
Brey, *Microprocessors and Peripherals: Hardware, Software, Interfacing, and Applications, 2nd Edition*, 0-675-20884-X
Gaonkar, *Microprocessor Architecture, Programming, and Applications with the 8085/8080A, 2nd Edition*, 0-675-20675-6
Gaonkar, *The Z80 Microprocessor: Architecture, Interfacing, Programming, and Design, 2nd Edition*, 0-02-340484-1
Goody, *Programming and Interfacing the 8086/8088 Microprocessor: A Product-Development Laboratory Process*, 0-675-21312-6
MacKenzie, *The 8051 Microcontroller*, 0-02-373650-X
Miller, *The 68000 Family of Microprocessors: Architecture, Programming, and Applications, 2nd Edition*, 0-02-381560-4
Quinn, *The 6800 Microprocessor*, 0-675-20515-8
Subbarao, *16/32 Bit Microprocessors: 68000/68010/68020 Software, Hardware, and Design Applications*, 0-675-21119-0

Electronic Communications

Monaco, *Introduction to Microwave Technology*, 0-675-21030-5
Monaco, *Preparing for the FCC Radio-Telephone Operator's License Examination*, 0-675-21313-4
Schoenbeck, *Electronic Communications: Modulation and Transmission, 2nd Edition*, 0-675-21311-8
Young, *Electronic Communication Techniques, 2nd Edition*, 0-675-21045-3
Zanger & Zanger, *Fiber Optics: Communication and Other Applications*, 0-675-20944-7

Microcomputer Servicing

Adamson, *Microcomputer Repair*, 0-02-300825-3
Asser, Stigliano, & Bahrenburg, *Microcomputer Servicing: Practical Systems and Troubleshooting, 2nd Edition*, 0-02-304241-9
Asser, Stigliano, & Bahrenburg, *Microcomputer Theory and Servicing, 2nd Edition*, 0-02-304231-1

Programming

Adamson, *Applied Pascal for Technology*, 0-675-20771-1
Adamson, *Structured BASIC Applied to Technology, 2nd Edition*, 0-02-300827-X
Adamson, *Structured C for Technology*, 0-675-20993-5
Adamson, *Structured C for Technology (with disk)*, 0-675-21289-8
Nashelsky & Boylestad, *BASIC Applied to Circuit Analysis*, 0-675-20161-6

Instrumentation and Measurement

Berlin & Getz, *Principles of Electronic Instrumentation and Measurement*, 0-675-20449-6
Buchla & McLachlan, *Applied Electronic Instrumentation and Measurement*, 0-675-21162-X
Gillies, *Instrumentation and Measurements for Electronic Technicians, 2nd Edition*, 0-02-343051-6

Transform Analysis

Kulathinal, *Transform Analysis and Electronic Networks with Applications*, 0-675-20765-7

Biomedical Equipment Technology

Aston, *Principles of Biomedical Instrumentation and Measurement*, 0-675-20943-9

Mathematics

Monaco, *Essential Mathematics for Electronics Technicians*, 0-675-21172-7
Davis, *Technical Mathematics*, 0-675-20338-4
Davis, *Technical Mathematics with Calculus*, 0-675-20965-X

INDUSTRIAL ELECTRONICS/INDUSTRIAL TECHNOLOGY

Bateson, *Introduction to Control System Technology, 4th Edition*, 0-02-306463-3
Fuller, *Robotics: Introduction, Programming, and Projects*, 0-675-21078-X
Goetsch, *Industrial Safety and Health: In the Age of High Technology*, 0-02-344207-7
Goetsch, *Industrial Supervision: In the Age of High Technology*, 0-675-22137-4
Horath, *Computer Numerical Control Programming of Machines*, 0-02-357201-9
Hubert, *Electric Machines: Theory, Operation, Applications, Adjustment, and Control*, 0-675-20765-7
Humphries, *Motors and Controls*, 0-675-20235-3
Hutchins, *Introduction to Quality: Management, Assurance, and Control*, 0-675-20896-3
Laviana, *Basic Computer Numerical Control Programming*, 0-675-21298-7
Reis, *Electronic Project Design and Fabrication, 2nd Edition*, 0-02-399230-1
Rosenblatt & Friedman, *Direct and Alternating Current Machinery, 2nd Edition*, 0-675-20160-8
Smith, *Statistical Process Control and Quality Improvement*, 0-675-21160-3
Webb, *Programmable Logic Controllers: Principles and Applications, 2nd Edition*, 0-02-424970-X
Webb & Greshock, *Industrial Control Electronics, 2nd Edition*, 0-02-424864-9

MECHANICAL/CIVIL TECHNOLOGY

Keyser, *Materials Science in Engineering, 4th Edition*, 0-675-20401-1
Kraut, *Fluid Mechanics for Technicians*, 0-675-21330-4
Mott, *Applied Fluid Mechanics, 3rd Edition*, 0-675-21026-7
Mott, *Machine Elements in Mechanical Design, 2nd Edition*, 0-675-22289-3
Rolle, *Thermodynamics and Heat Power, 3rd Edition*, 0-675-21016-X
Spiegel & Limbrunner, *Applied Statics and Strength of Materials*, 0-675-21123-9
Wolansky & Akers, *Modern Hydraulics: The Basics at Work*, 0-675-20987-0
Wolf, *Statics and Strength of Materials: A Parallel. Approach to Understanding Structures*, 0-675-20622-7

DRAFTING TECHNOLOGY

Cooper, *Introduction to VersaCAD*, 0-675-21164-6
Goetsch & Rickman, *Computer-Aided Drafting with AutoCAD*, 0-675-20915-3
Kirkpatrick & Kirkpatrick, *AutoCAD for Interior Design and Space Planning*, 0-02-364455-9
Kirkpatrick, *The AutoCAD Book: Drawing, Modeling, and Applications, 2nd Edition*, 0-675-22288-5
Kirkpatrick, *The AutoCAD Book: Drawing, Modeling, and Applications Including Version 12, 3rd Edition*, 0-02-364440-0
Lamit & Lloyd, *Drafting for Electronics, 2nd Edition*, 0-02-367342-7
Lamit & Paige, *Computer-Aided Design and Drafting*, 0-675-20475-5
Maruggi, *Technical Graphics: Electronics Worktext, 2nd Edition*, 0-675-21378-9
Maruggi, *The Technology of Drafting*, 0-675-20762-2
Sell, *Basic Technical Drawing*, 0-675-21001-1

TECHNICAL WRITING

Croft, *Getting a Job: Resume Writing, Job Application Letters, and Interview Strategies*, 0-675-20917-X
Panares, *A Handbook of English for Technical Students*, 0-675-20650-2
Pfeiffer, *Proposal Writing: The Art of Friendly Persuasion*, 0-675-20988-9
Pfeiffer, *Technical Writing: A Practical Approach*, 0-675-21221-9
Roze, *Technical Communications: The Practical Craft*, 0-675-20641-3
Weisman, *Basic Technical Writing, 6th Edition*, 0-675-21256-1

Preface

This workbook is designed as a companion to Lamit and Lloyd's *Drafting for Electronics,* Second Edition. General drafting information discussed in Chapters 1–7, Chapter 9, and Chapter 19 of that text can be used to complete the assignments in the workbook.

The second edition of the workbook incorporates changes made in the second edition of the text. Many new plates and two new sections, "Programmable Controllers and Robotics" (Chapter 15) and "Power Distribution" (Chapter 16), have been added. Also, a discussion of surface-mounted printed circuit boards is presented. A table of contents has been added for this edition.

Chapters 1–7 and Chapter 9 of the text are devoted to aspects of electronics and mechanical drafting that provide the student with a general background. Basic layout methods, standards and specifications, and drafting conventions for all types of electronics drawings are presented. Discussions of equipment, linework, lettering, dimensioning, projections, designations, and general electronics theory help students understand the "application" chapters (Chapter 8 and Chapters 10–18). Various types of electronics drawings and typical projects from industry are presented in this workbook. Students can follow the related chapter and use the text appendices as they complete the workbook assignments.

The workbook assignments are divided into those that use A size worksheets (Plates provided in the second part) and those problems to be completed on B or C size formats (Projects). Each plate and project can be completed using a variety of methods. Pencil, ink, or computer-aided drafting (CAD) can be used to draw the problem, depending on the availability of equipment. Transfer symbols, preprinted component outlines, and conductor tape should be assigned for a few of the plates, especially in the printed circuit board section. Drafting templates should be used for all diagrams assigned.

Since CAD stations are becoming more available, many of the projects and plates can be adapted to a CAD electronics drafting and design class. The instructor who has access to a CAD system may choose to have students construct each plate on a larger format instead of the given A size. The workbook will then become a problem book, and the worksheets can be used to sketch preliminary and trial layouts for each assignment.

General instructions presented at the beginning of the workbook apply to all problems in this workbook. Each section then begins with specific directions or information needed to complete the assignments in it. By referring to the table of contents, students can easily locate a topic and related problems.

A solutions manual is available from the publisher. Note that many of the problems can have several "right answers" especially in the printed circuit board section. The instructor must determine the acceptability of these answers.

The authors would gratefully appreciate any feedback from instructors or students concerning this workbook. Criticisms, changes, corrections, or specific new ideas are welcome and encouraged. The authors will answer all letters.

Contents

Instructions

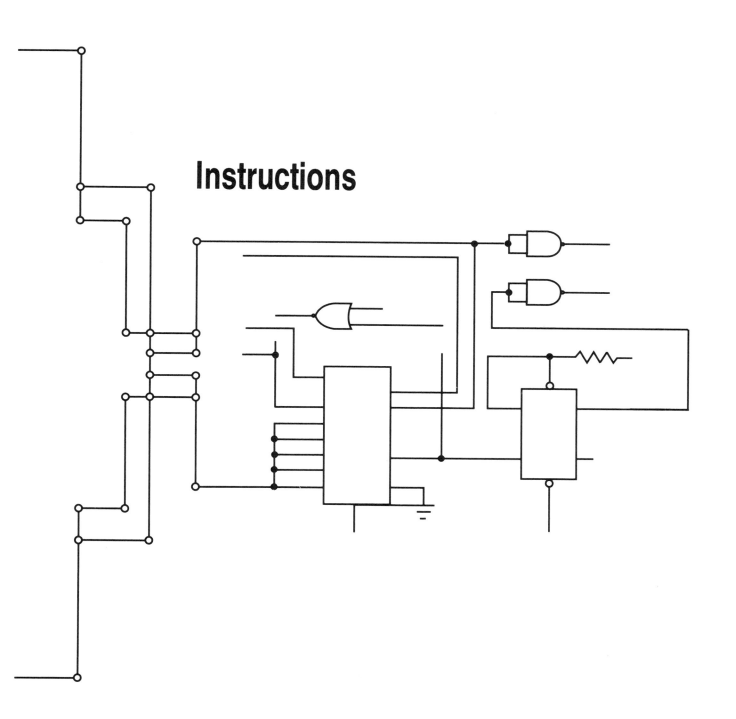

GENERAL INSTRUCTIONS

Each assignment in this workbook can be completed using manual methods of pencil, inking, or dry transfer symbols and preprinted component outlines. CAD may also be assigned for selected problems depending on the availability of a system. The instructor must decide which plates or projects are to be in each medium. The authors suggest a balanced approach of all methods to give the student a variety of experiences in the laying out and the drafting of electronic and electromechanical projects.

A trial sketch should be used for every problem regardless of the methods used to complete the assignment. Sketching paper or onionskin may be laid over the workbook plates and the trial sketch lightly penciled in. When using CAD, the sketch may be digitized directly.

Drafting templates are required for all diagrams and components when using the manual methods. Unless specified differently by the instructor, all projects are to be drawn using mechanical equipment and completed as finished drafting projects to industry standards. The linework and lettering must be dark and neatly executed. Problems should be kept clean and neat.

A 10 × 10 grid underlay is provided at the end of the workbook and can be used for the workbook plates if a light board is available. Worksheets begin on page 99. Lettering will be between ⅛ in. (3 mm) and 5/32 in. (4 mm) high. The student should concentrate on vertical lettering for a majority of the problems. A few of the diagram problems can be completed with inclined lettering. Refer to the text's appendices for symbols, designations, and other background information.

Components and Symbols

(See Chapter 8.)

Plates 1–5. Draw each electronic component symbol three times. The POWER TRANSFORMER on Plate 3 should be drawn only once. Place the reference designation, value, tolerance, voltage, and/or power rating according to accepted practice. Use an electronics template corresponding to ANSI Y32.2, .200 in. grid. Lettering is to be 5/32 in. (4 mm).

Plates 6 and 7. Using a template, draw each logic symbol two times. Include the gate identification and the pin numbers for each. Use a logic template corresponding to ANSI Y32.14, ½ size (MIL-STD-806C). Lettering is to be ⅛ in. (3.1 mm) and 5/32 in. (4 mm).

Plates 8 and 9. Draw the required component outlines one time next to or below the given sketch. Note the case style and pin identification. Use a 2X scale component outline template corresponding to Bishop Graphics' Catalog number 3367 and 3368 or equivalent.

Schematic Diagrams

(See Chapter 10.)

Construct each diagram with ELECTRICAL AND ELECTRONIC SYMBOLS template by RapiDesign or equivalent (ANSI Y32.2, .200 in. grid). Transfer symbols (or CAD) may also be assigned for any of the following schematic drawings (Plates and Projects). Lettering is to be 5/32 in. (4 mm). Provide all designations and draw all symbols as per standards. Draw each schematic diagram using specifications from Chapter 10. Where missing, incomplete, or not to the appropriate standards, assign the proper values and designations.

4

Plate 10. Use the schematic of the HIGH-SPEED AN-ALOG COMPARATOR shown in Figure 1. This schematic will be used for the analog circuit board required for Plate 73 in the PCB problem section.

FIGURE 1

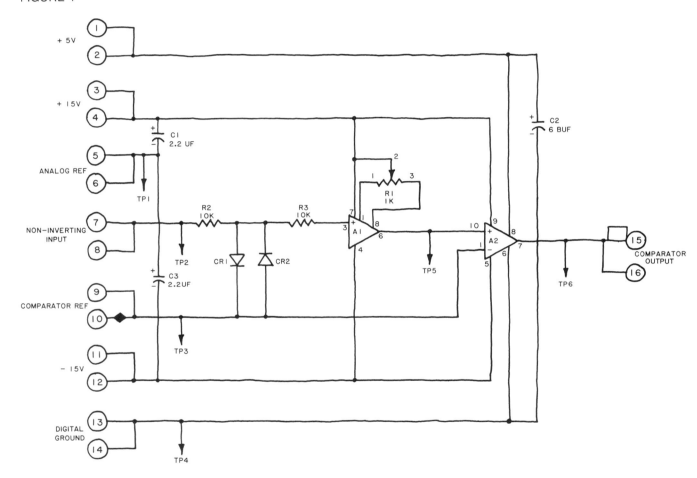

Plate 11. Draw the schematic diagram for the DUAL SCHMITT TRIGGERS shown in Figure 2. This schematic is to be used for Plate 74 in the PCB section. Draw only the portion started on the workbook plate (the right side) because the total drawing will not fit the format. Note that the instructor may assign the complete drawing to be done on a C size sheet.

FIGURE 2

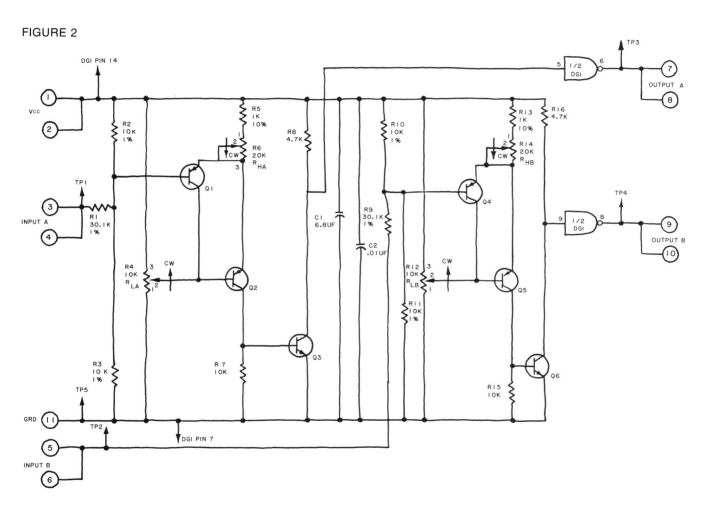

6

Plate 12. Draw the schematic of the BUFFER AMPLI-
FIER shown in Figure 3. Plate 12 will be used for the
printed circuit board package documentation for Plate
75.

FIGURE 3

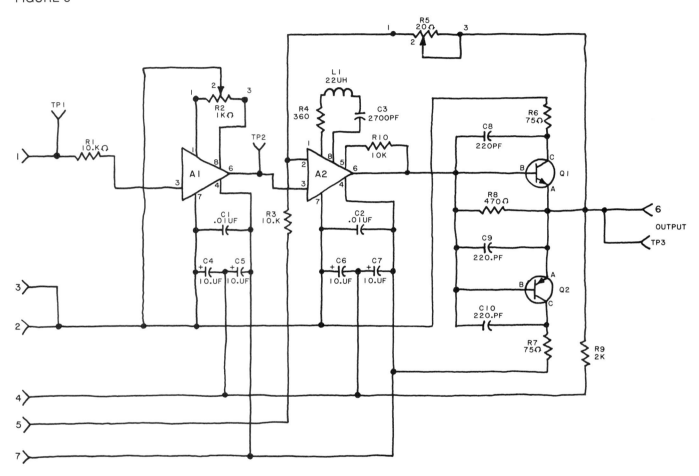

Plate 13. Construct the schematic diagram of the UNI-VERSAL OPERATIONAL AMPLIFIER shown in Figure 4. Draw only the center and the right side of the diagram because the space is limited. Show from R1 to the OUTPUTS.

FIGURE 4

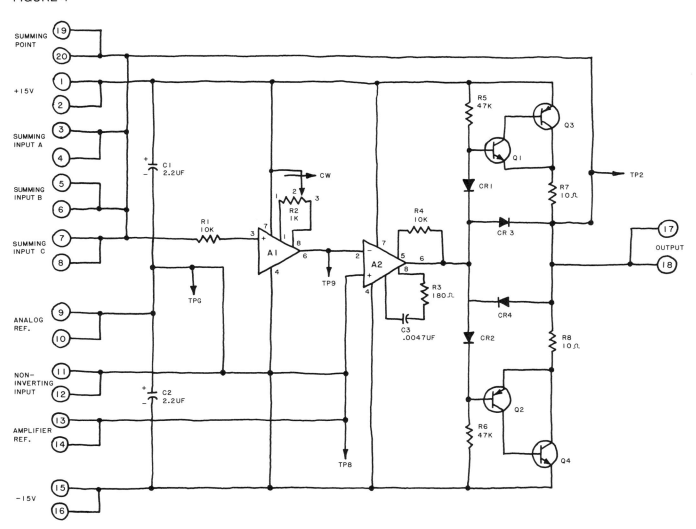

8

Plate 14. Using the schematic diagram sketch of the
SAMPLE AND HOLD AMPLIFIER shown in Figure
5, redraw the project on the provided A size plate.

FIGURE 5

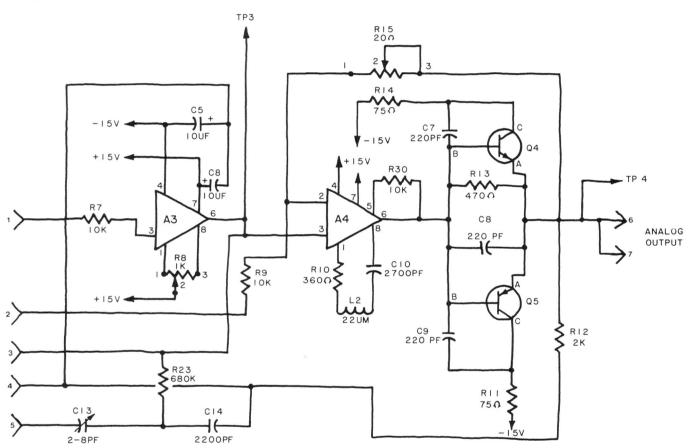

Plate 15. Draw the schematic diagram of the VOLT-AGE REGULATOR using a differential operational amplifier in Figure 6. Use the general specifications provided, but use a .250 in. grid ANSI Y32.2 electronics template.

FIGURE 6

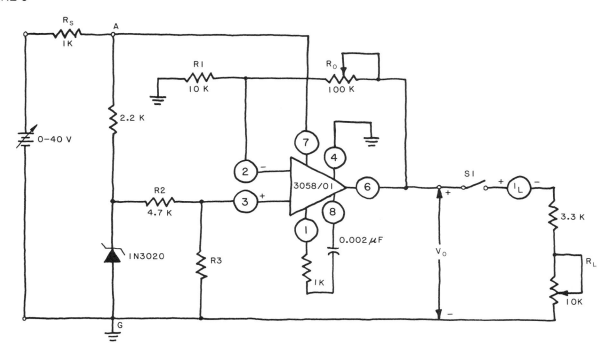

Plate 16. Draw the diagram of the 2 KV NEGATIVE POWER SUPPLY (Figure 7) using transfer symbols or a template. This diagram is to be used for the PCB problem shown for Plate 76.

FIGURE 7

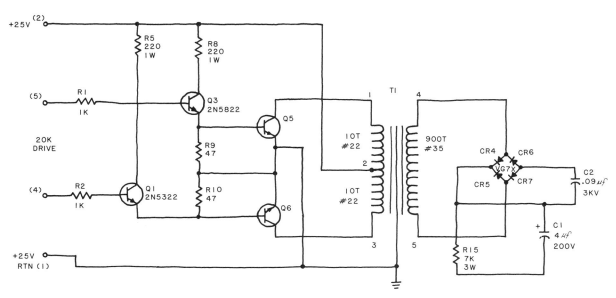

Plate 17. Draw the diagram of the DIGITAL FRE-QUENCY METER shown in Figure 8. Assign your own reference designations to all components.

FIGURE 8

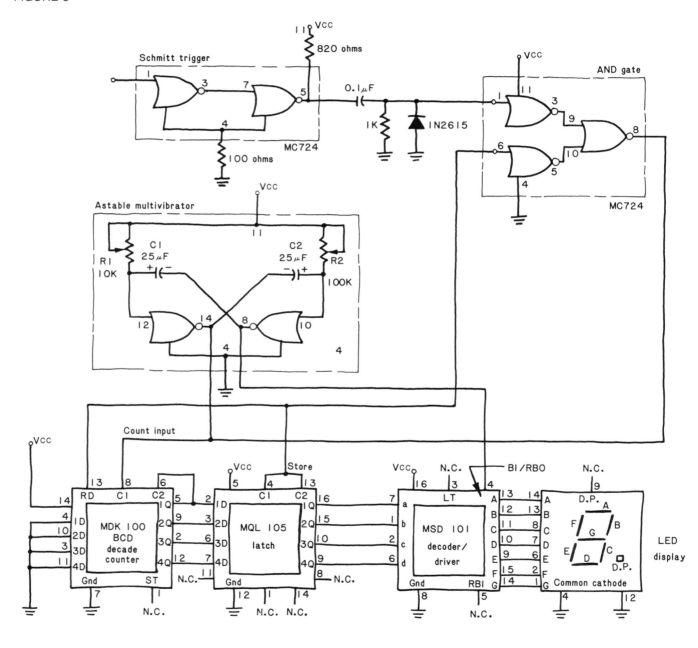

Plate 18. Draw the circuit shown in Figure 9.

FIGURE 9

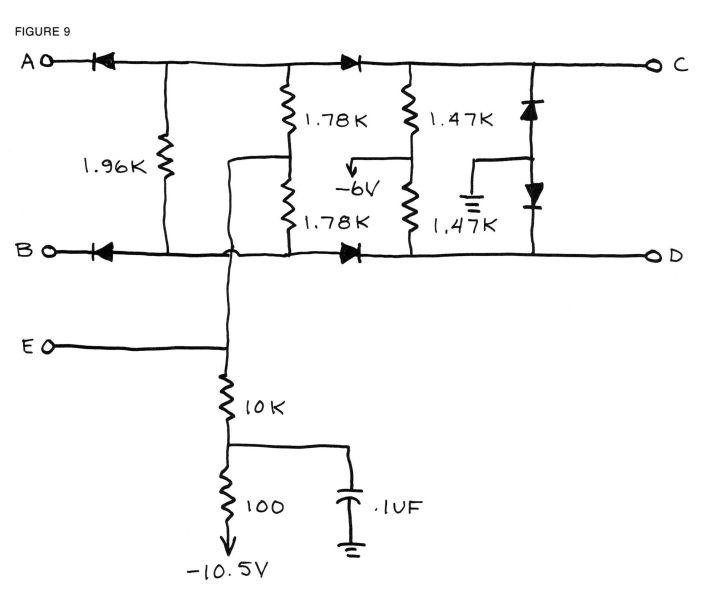

Plate 19. Draw the discrete component circuit schematic provided in Figure 10. Use the schematic to create a PCB using SMDs for Project 34.

FIGURE 10

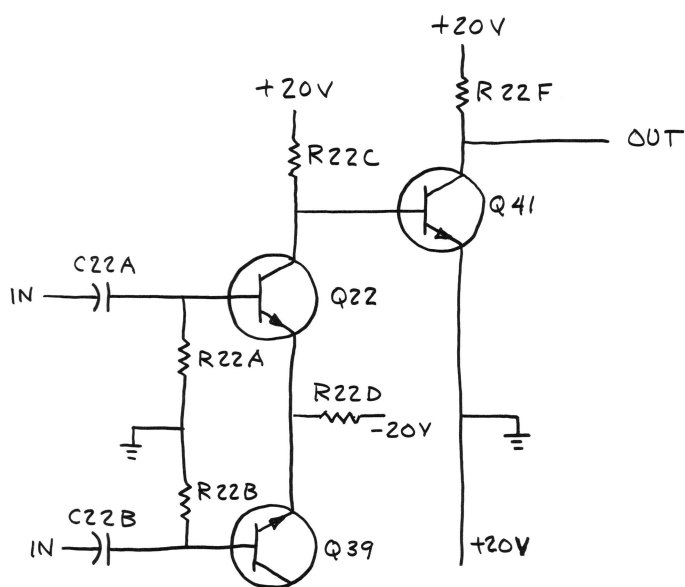

Plate 20. Draw the DZJ circuit shown in Figure 11.

FIGURE 11

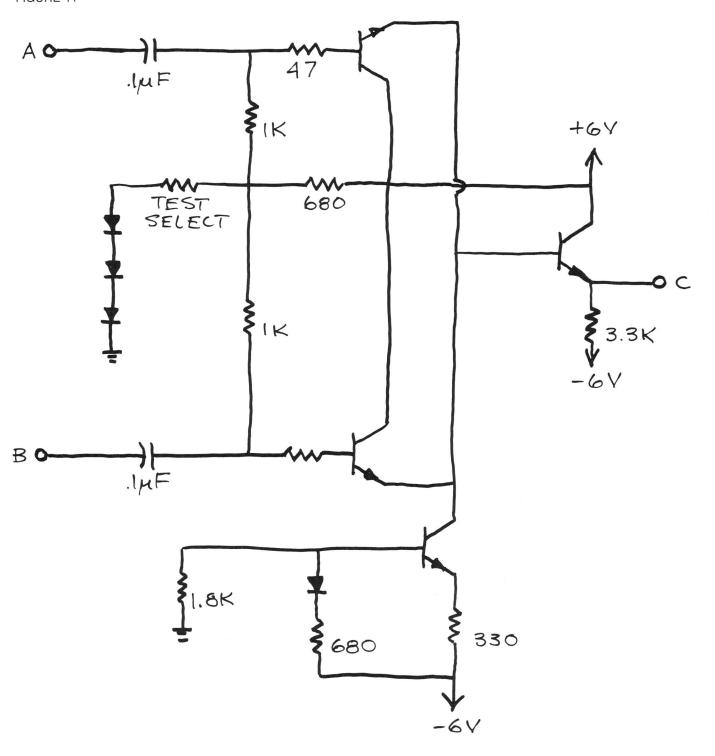

14

Plate 21. Draw Figure 12 (series regulator using paralleled transistors and amplification of voltage variations) as shown. Use the diagram to create a PCB with SMDs as per Project 35.

FIGURE 12

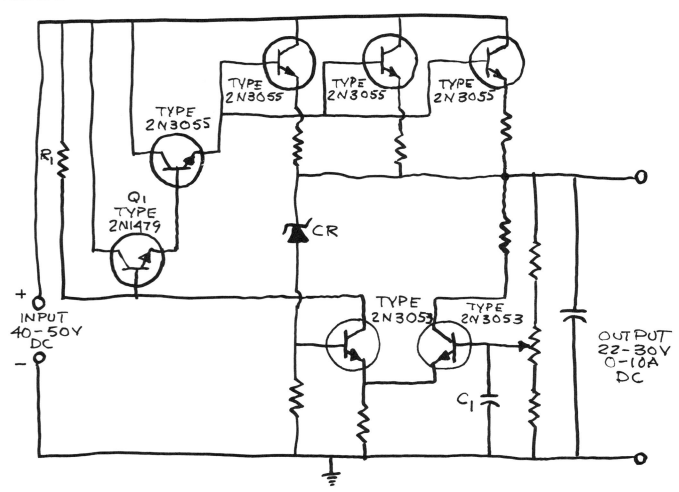

Plate 22. Draw the USD delay circuit shown in Figure 13.

FIGURE 13

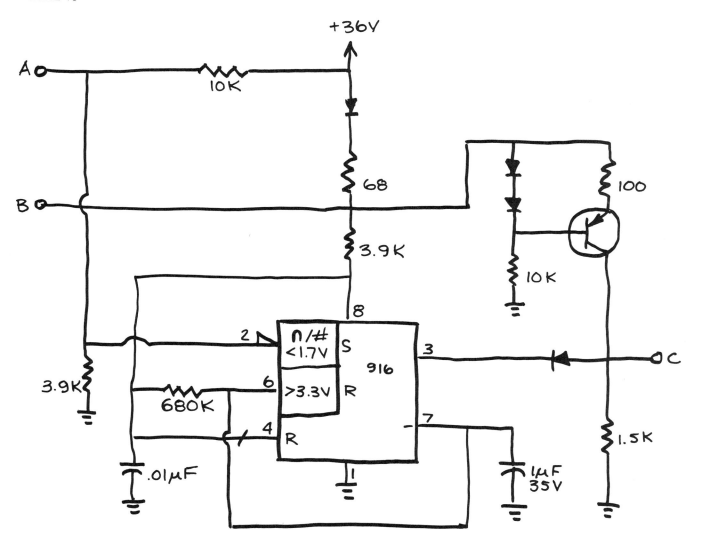

Project 1. Draw the circuit shown in Figure 14 on a B
size sheet.

FIGURE 14

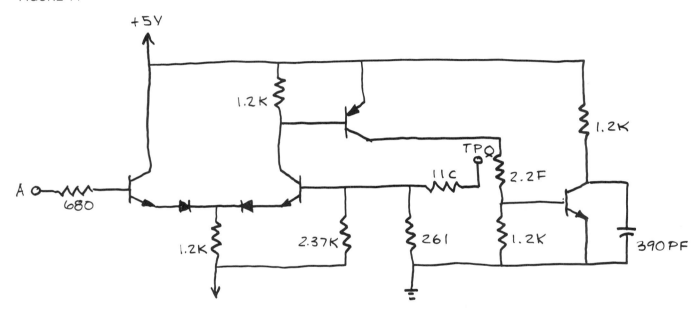

Project 2. Draw the schematic of the EXTERNAL
CLOCK GENERATOR shown in Figure 15.

FIGURE 15

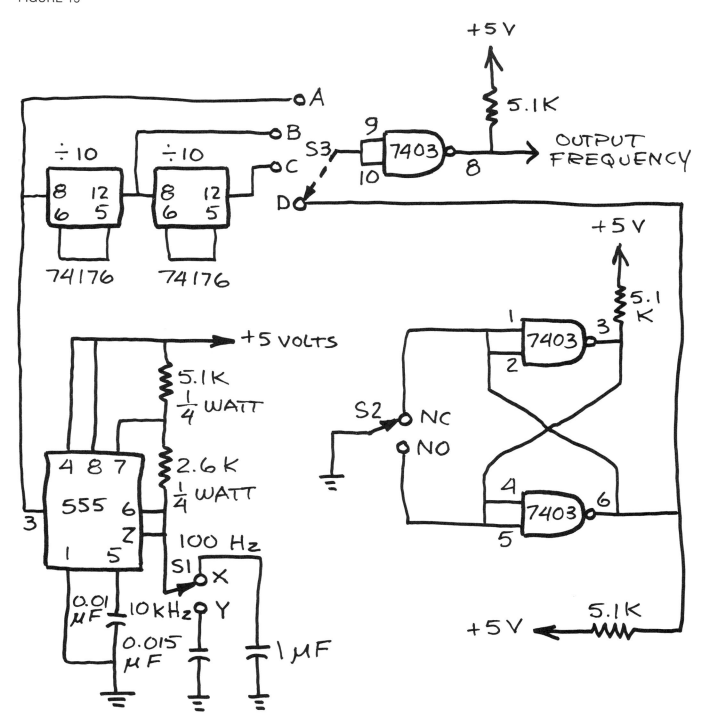

Project 3. Draw the VERTICAL DEFLECTION CIR-
CUIT provided in Figure 16. Use the schematic to lay
out a PCB with SMDs for Project 36.

FIGURE 16

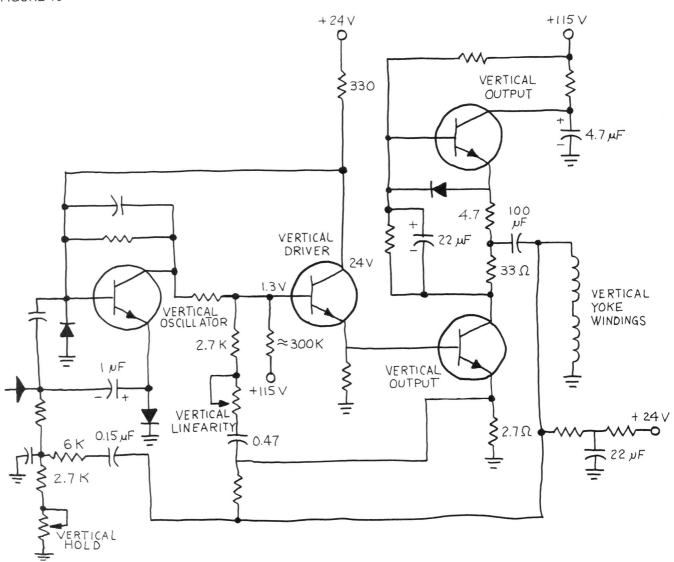

Project 4. Draw the schematic of the BATTERY
CHARGER with a bridge rectifier shown in Figure 17.

FIGURE 17

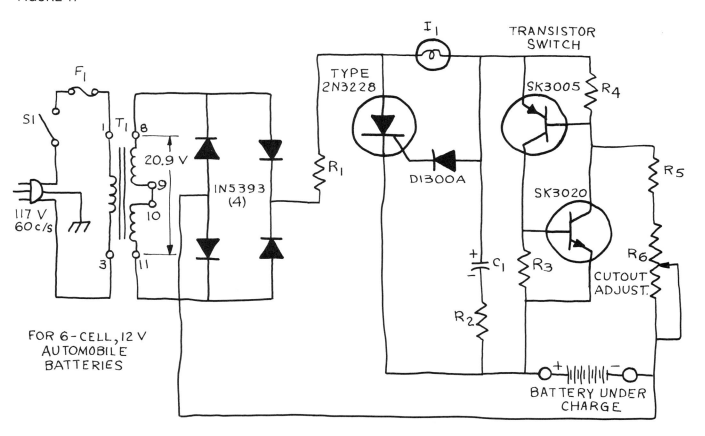

Project 5. Draw the schematic shown in Figure 18. Use correct designations and numbering of components.

FIGURE 18

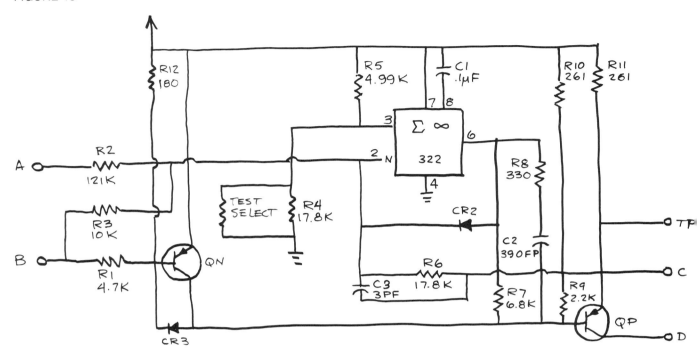

Project 6. Draw the schematic in Figure 19.

FIGURE 19

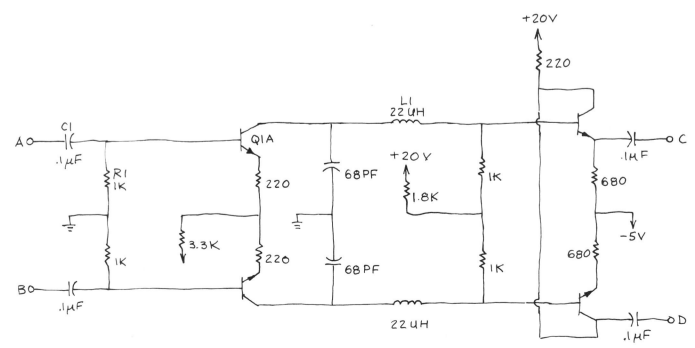

Project 7. Draw the schematic in Figure 20.

FIGURE 20

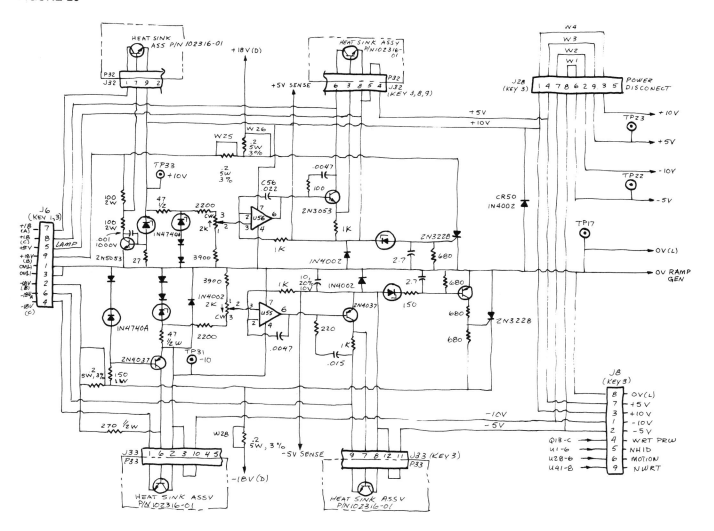

Block Diagrams

(See Chapter 11.)

Construct the diagrams of this section using specifications provided in Chapter 11 of the text. If available, use the standard block diagram template to construct the geometric shapes. Letter the function nomenclature with vertical 5/32 in. (4 mm) or 1/8 in. (3 mm) lettering. Center the callouts within each block shape. Use the plate's available space to layout the diagram without crowding the shapes.

Plate 23. Draw the block diagram of the complex functions performed by the 31-TRANSISTOR MC-1305 using the sketch shown in Figure 21.

FIGURE 21

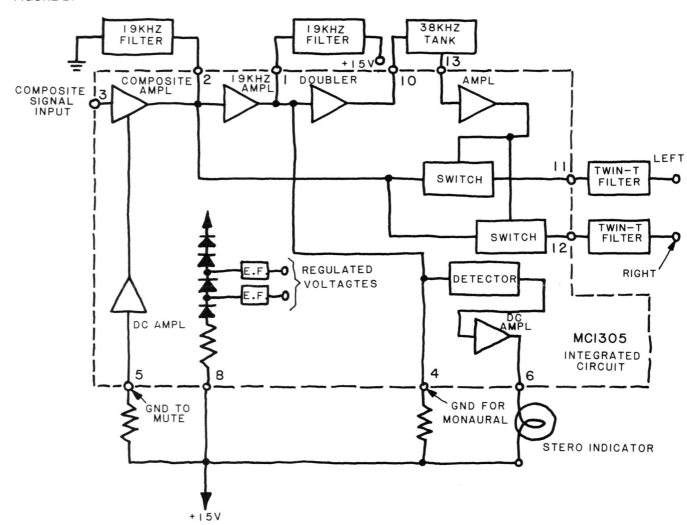

Plate 24. Using the block diagram sketch of the TELE-COMMUNICATIONS SYSTEM in Figure 22, draw the block diagram.

FIGURE 22

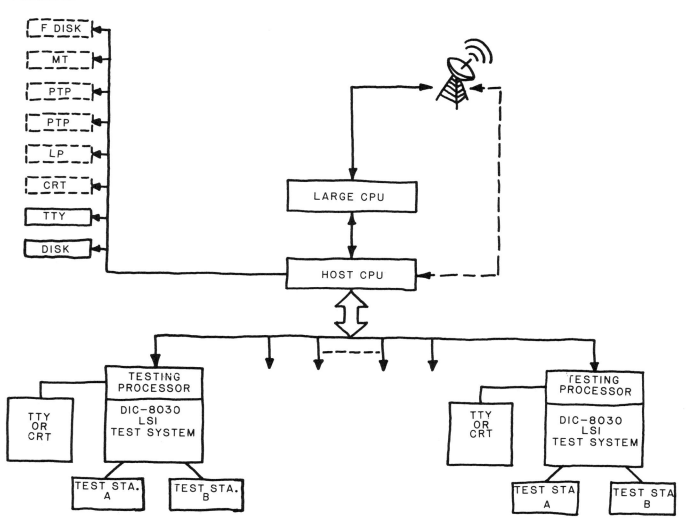

Plate 25. Draw the FUNCTIONAL BLOCK DIA-
GRAM shown as a sketch in Figure 23.

FIGURE 23

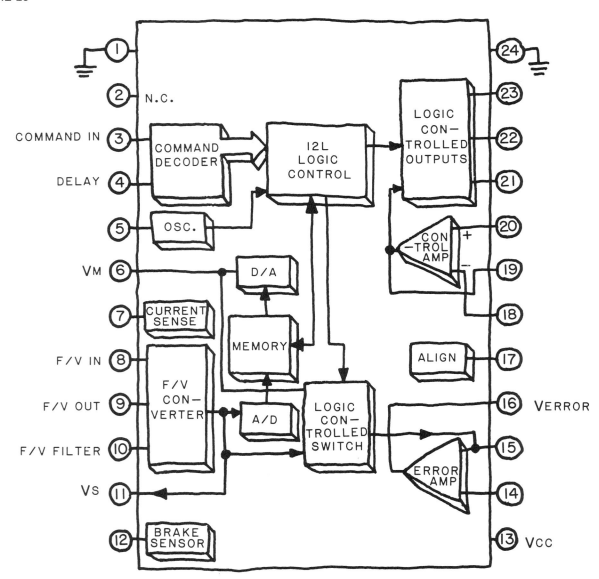

Plate 26. Lay out the flowchart for the DATA ANA-LYZER in Figure 24. Use the "Timesaver" template #811 corresponding to ANSI 3.5–1970 if one is available. Use appropriate size lettering to match the call-outs already provided.

FIGURE 24

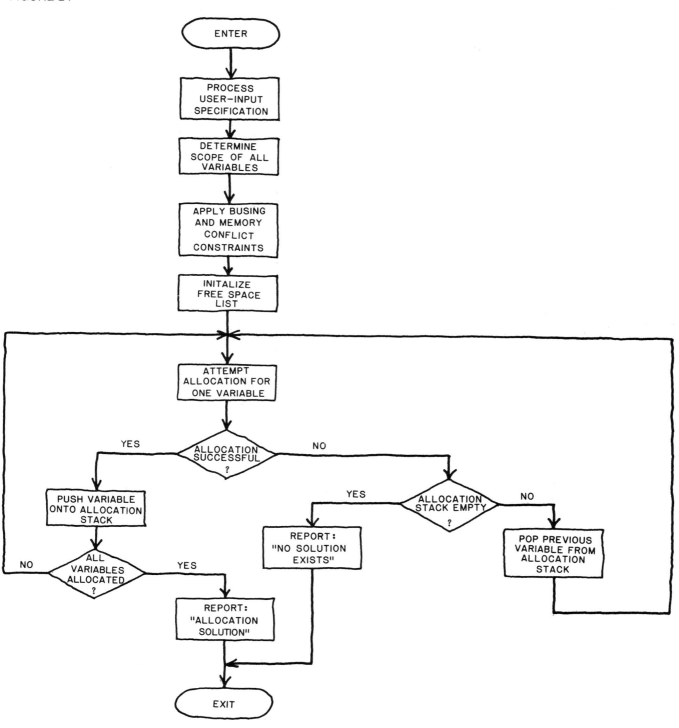

Plate 27. Draw the flowchart of the MONITOR PRO-GRAM in Figure 25. This is a computer block diagram, and a standard flowcharting template should be used if one is available. Draw only down to *DISPLAY MODE* and *TEST SYSTEM PORT*. Figure 25 can be assigned as a complete block diagram using a B or C size sheet.

FIGURE 25

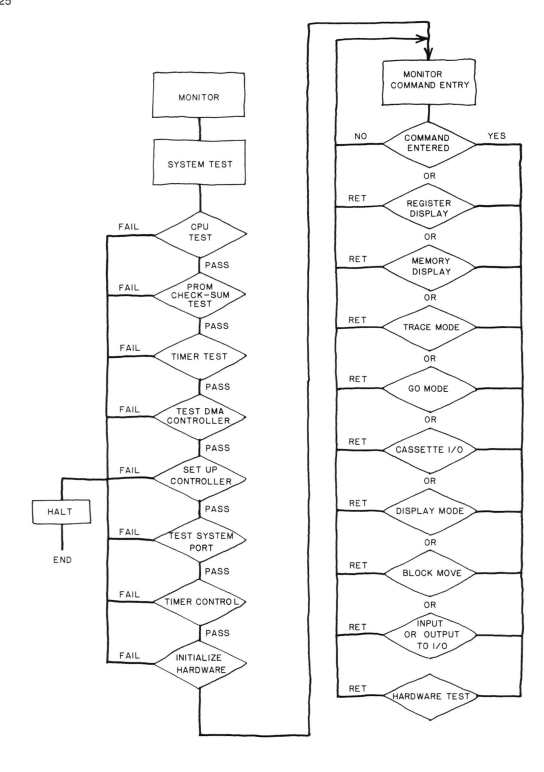

Plate 28. Draw the MAGNETIC-BUBBLE TEST SYSTEM diagrammed in Figure 26.

FIGURE 26

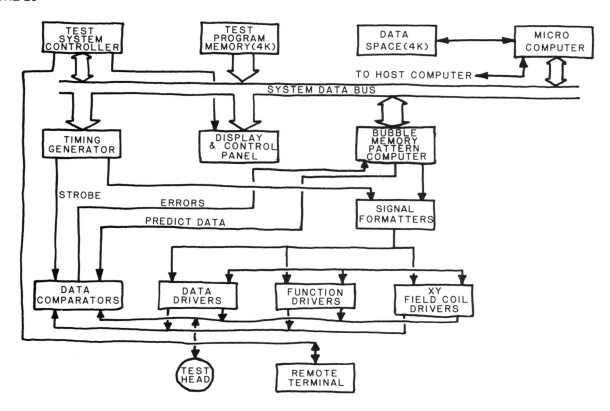

Plate 29. Using the block diagram of the AMPLIFIER SYSTEM in Figure 27, draw the diagram horizontally on the page.

FIGURE 27

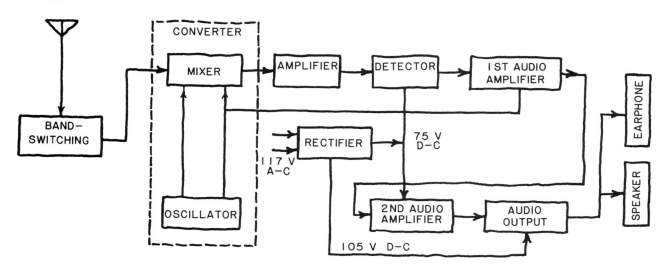

Plate 30. Draw the DRIVE FUNCTIONAL block diagram shown in Figure 28.

FIGURE 28

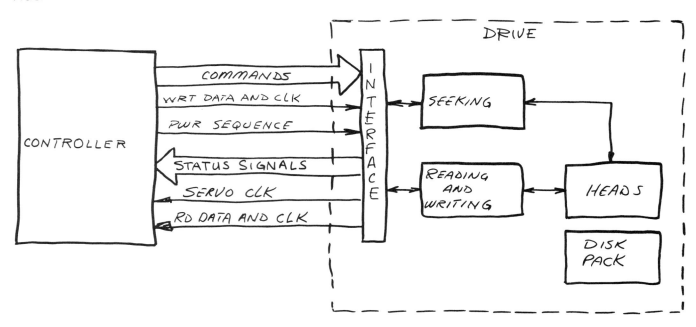

Plate 31. Draw the WRITE CIRCUITS block diagram provided in Figure 29.

FIGURE 29

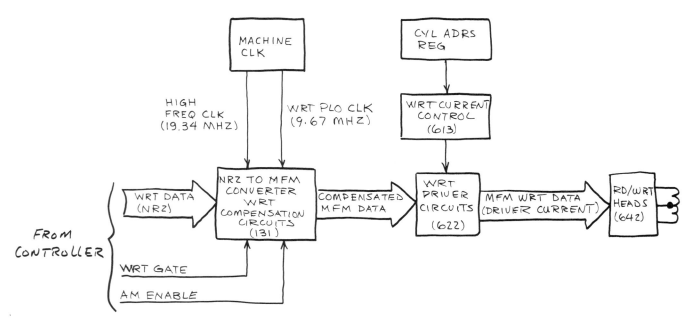

Plate 32. Draw the READ/WRITE CIRCUIT block diagram given in Figure 30.

FIGURE 30

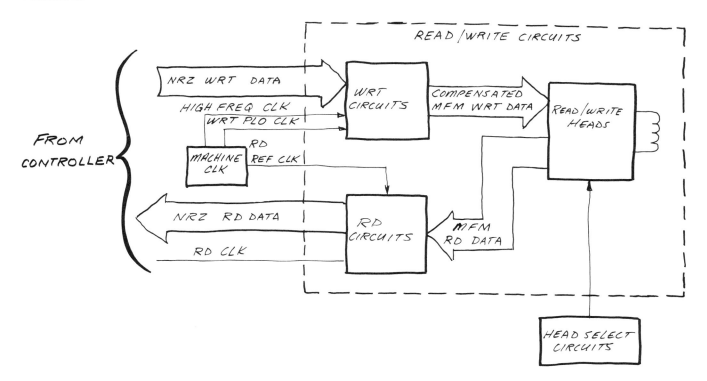

Project 8. Draw the HI-FI AMPLIFIER diagram (Figure 31) on a B size sheet.

FIGURE 31

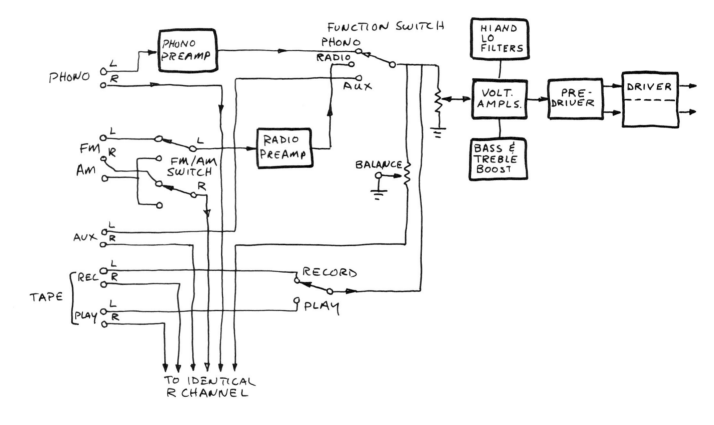

Project 9. Draw the RESERVE flowchart shown in Figure 32.

FIGURE 32

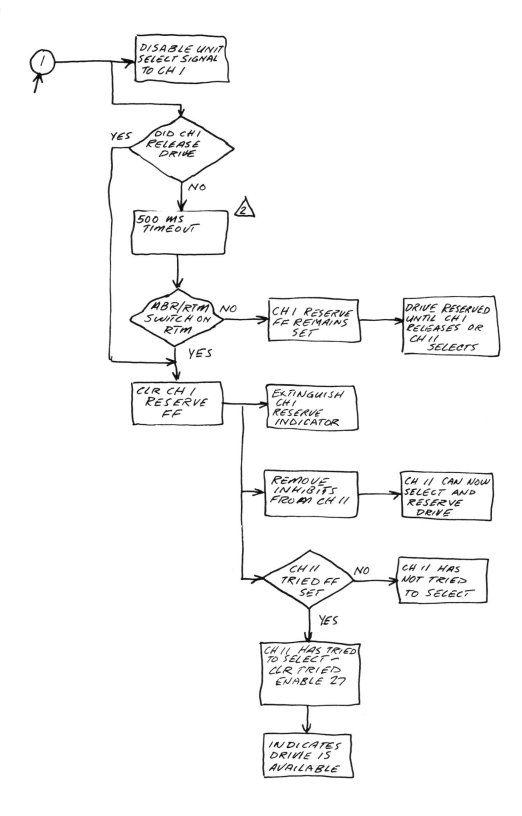

Project 10. Draw the TRACK SERVO circuit in Figure 33.

FIGURE 33

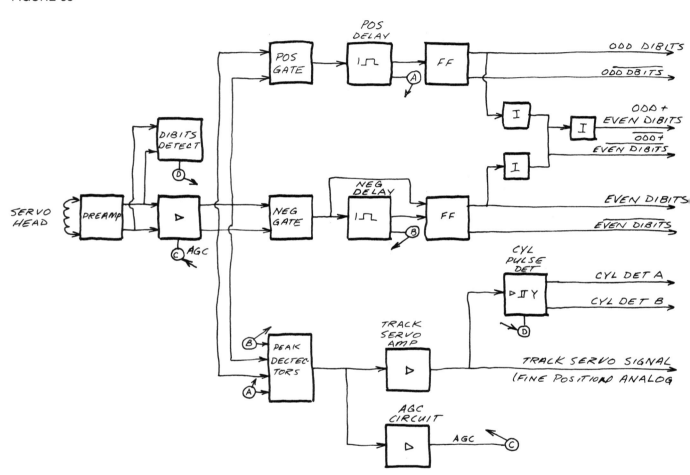

Logic Diagrams

(See Chapter 12.)

Use MIL-STD-806C or ANSI STD Y32.14 template. Note the template scale will vary with the plate, 1:4, 1:2 or full scale. Use ⅛ in. (3 mm) and ⁵⁄₃₂ in. (4 mm) lettering. Plates in the logic section make excellent assignments to be completed on a CAD system because many elements of each diagram repeat. The stu-dent will get to practice creating entities that need to be *MOVED* and *COPIED*. Assign proper values and designations where missing or incomplete.

Plate 33. Lay out the logic diagram of the 16 × 2 IN-PUT NAND GATES–DTL circuit sketched in Figure 34. Draw only OG1 and OG2 and the power supply. The instructor may assign this project to be completed on a C size sheet showing the total drawing. This diagram will be used as the diagram for laying out the digital printed circuit board problem shown in Plate 78.

FIGURE 34

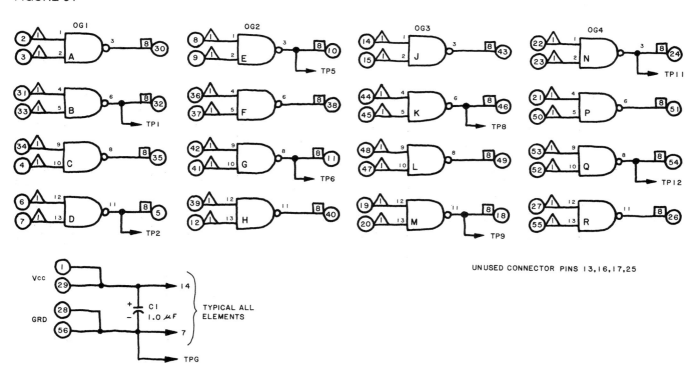

UNUSED CONNECTOR PINS 13,16,17,25

Plate 34. Draw the logic diagram for the 8 × 4 INPUT CAPACITY DRIVER NAND GATES–DTL circuit shown in Figure 35. Draw only gates A, B, C, and D and the power supply. This logic diagram will be used for the printed circuit problem shown in Plate 79. Template size will be full scale.

FIGURE 35

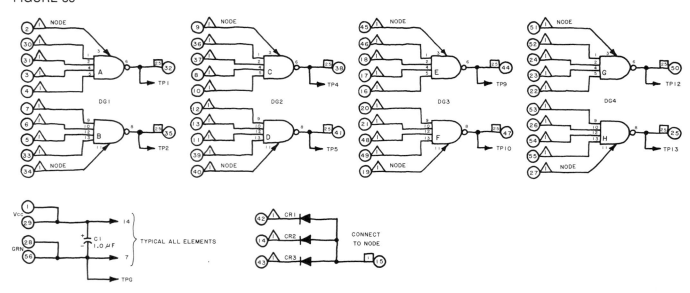

Plate 35. Lay out the SIX FORM "A" REED RELAYS WITH 3-INPUT DRIVERS–DTL circuit diagram shown in Figure 36. Draw only gates A, B, and C, and the power supply. This plate will be used for the printed circuit problem documentation for Plate 80. The instructor may assign the total logic diagram to be completed on a B or C size sheet. Use a full-scale size template.

FIGURE 36

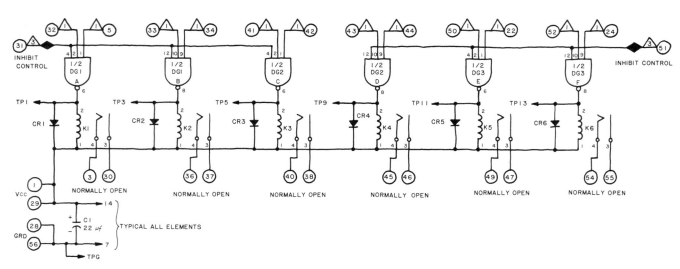

Plate 36. Draw the TWELVE-BIT SHIFT REGISTER W/GATED PARALLEL ENTRY–DTL diagram shown in Figure 37. Draw only the parallel data input for OG1 and T FF1 in the "A" portion of the diagram. A complete diagram can be assigned for a B size project. Use a full-scale size template. This diagram will be used for the printed circuit problem in Plate 81.

FIGURE 37

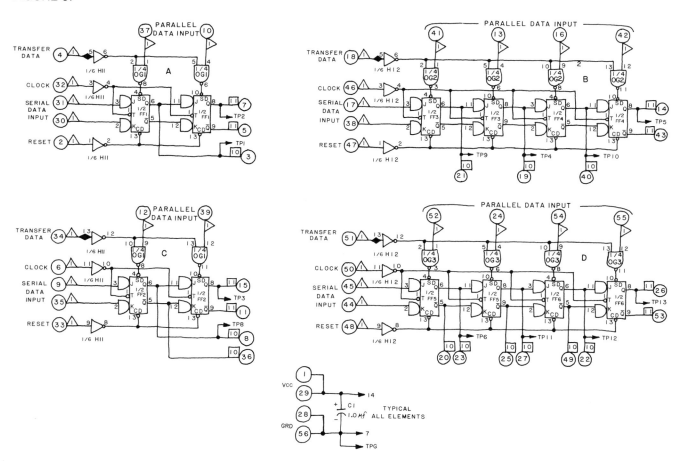

Plate 37. Lay out the diagram for the single-sided board shown in Figure 38. The FLASHER CIRCUIT will also be used for the printed circuit board problem for Plate 77.

FIGURE 38

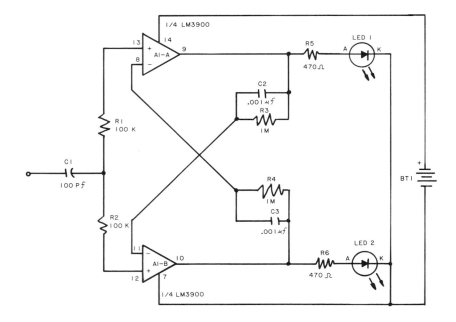

Plate 38. Draw the diagram for the CLOCK STORAGE–DTL in Figure 39. This diagram is to be used for the printed circuit board problem for Plate 82. Each integrated circuit should have a decoupler capacitor.

FIGURE 39

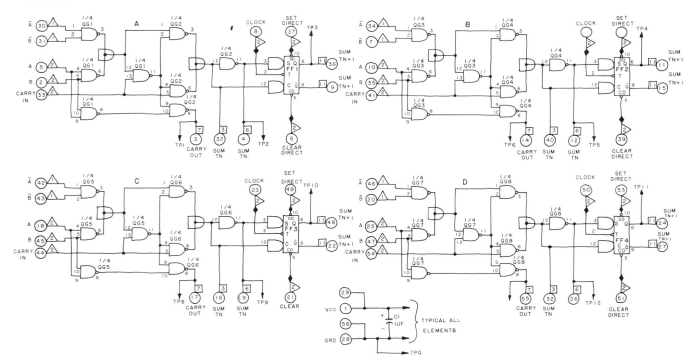

Plate 39. Draw the diagram for the LINE DRIVER WITH 3-WIRE COMPLEMENTARY OUTPUT– DTL shown in Figure 40. Include the power supply on this assignment. Template is full scale.

FIGURE 40

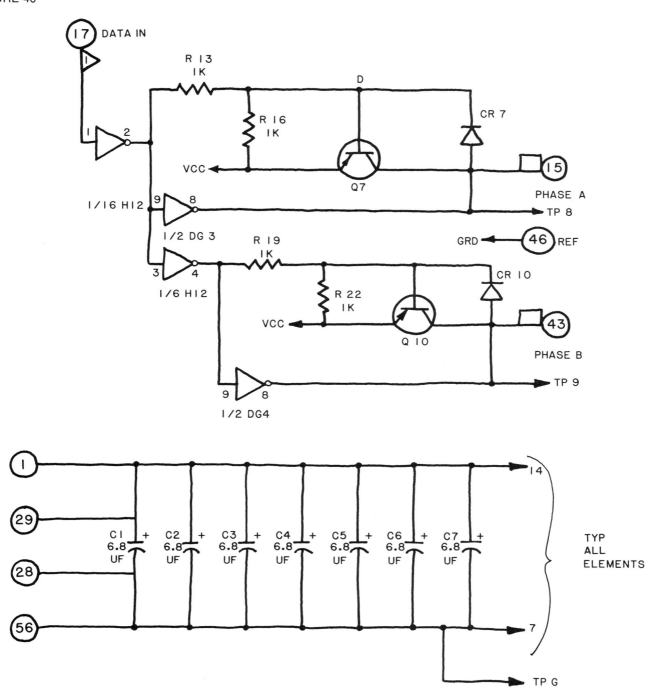

38

Plate 40. Draw the diagram for the 16-BIT RANDOM
ACCESS MEMORY shown in Figure 41.

FIGURE 41

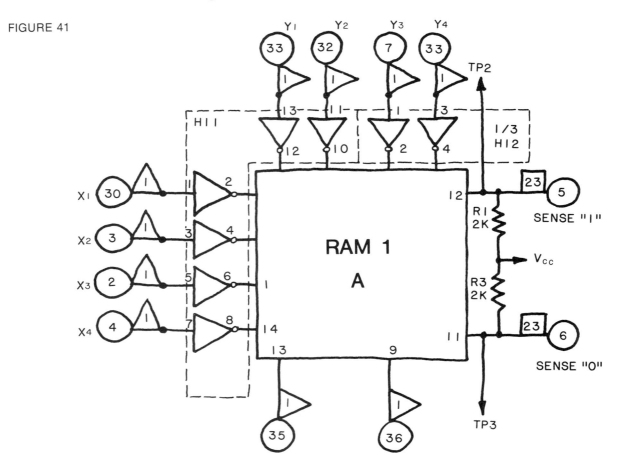

Project 11. On a C size sheet, draw the BASIC PAR-
ALLEL BINARY ADDER-SUBTRACTER UNIT
shown in Figure 42.

FIGURE 42

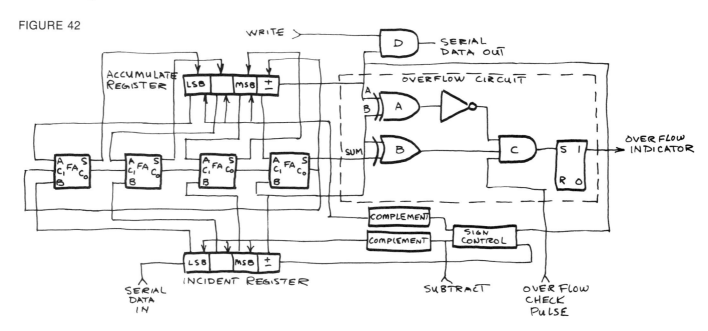

Project 12. Draw the SINGLE-CHANNEL UNIT SE-
LECT logic diagram (Figure 43) on a C size sheet.

FIGURE 43

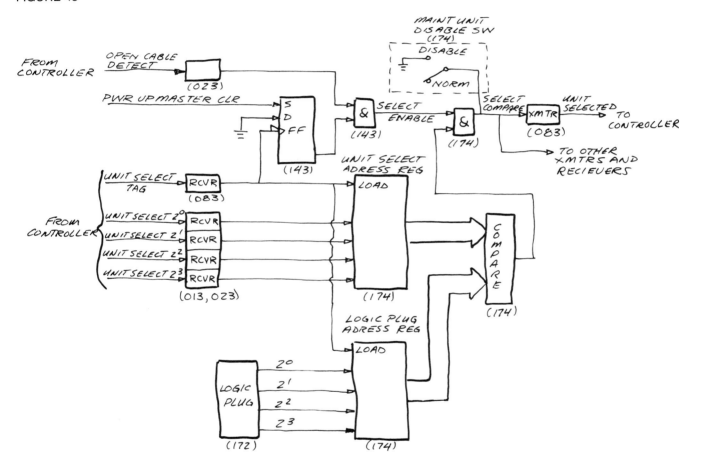

Project 13. Draw the logic diagram shown in Figure 44.

FIGURE 44

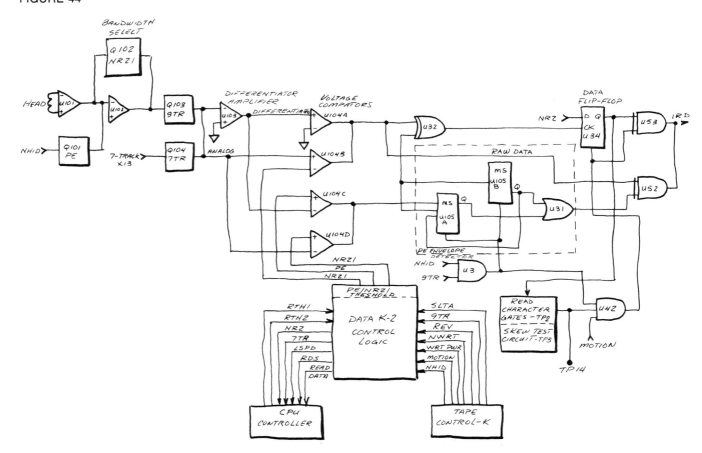

Project 14. Draw the DECADE COUNTER provided in Figure 45.

FIGURE 45

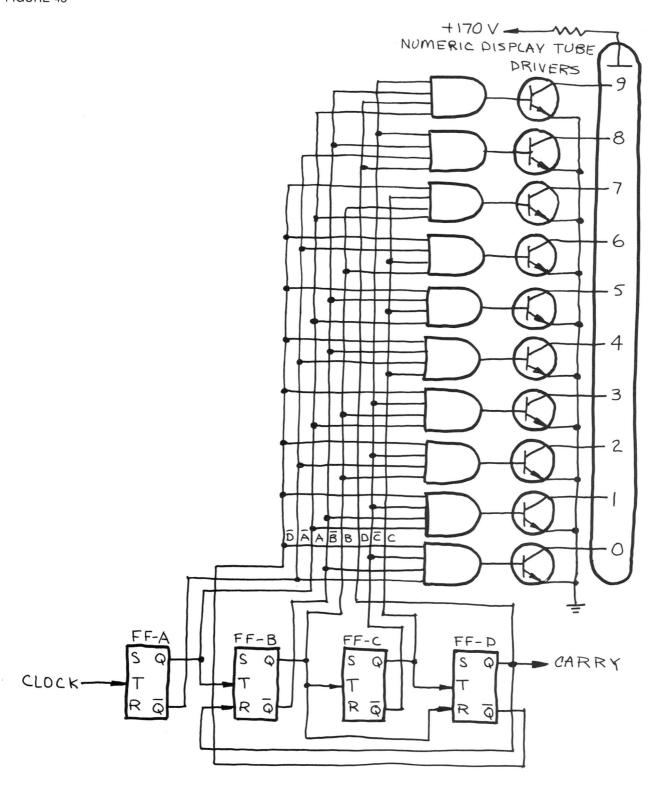

Project 15. Draw the diagram given in Figure 46.

FIGURE 46

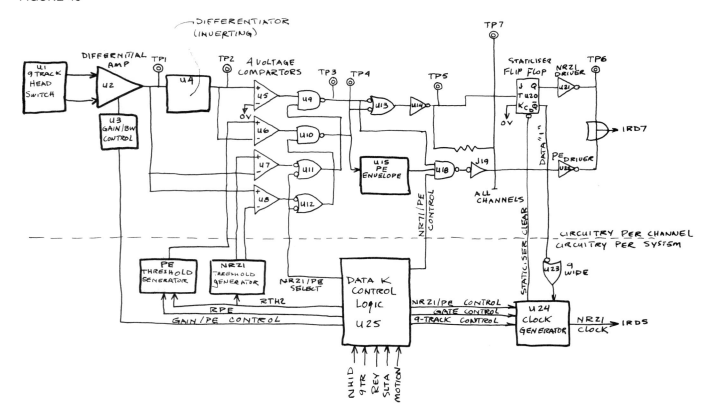

Wiring Diagrams

(See Chapter 13.)

Use ⁵⁄₃₂ in. (4 mm) lettering on all projects in this section. Lay out the assignments to make optimum use of the limited space. Use specifications provided in Chapter 13 and the appendices of the text.

Plate 41. Draw the wiring diagram of the CONTROL PANEL shown in Figure 47.

FIGURE 47

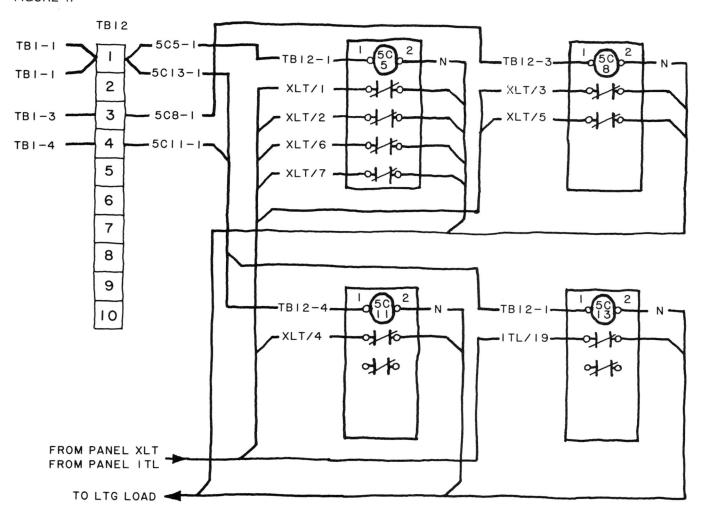

Plate 42. Complete the WIRE HARNESS ASSEM-
BLY shown in Figure 48.

FIGURE 48

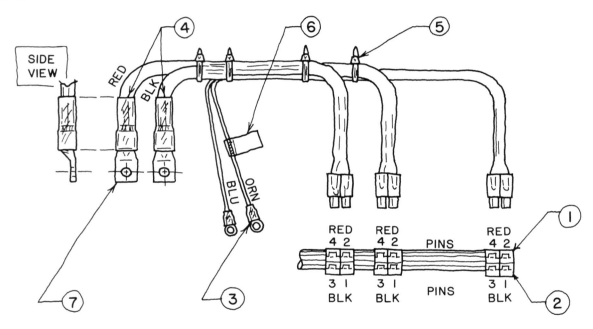

Plate 43. Lay out the diagram of the H.V. SWITCH sketched in Figure 49.

FIGURE 49

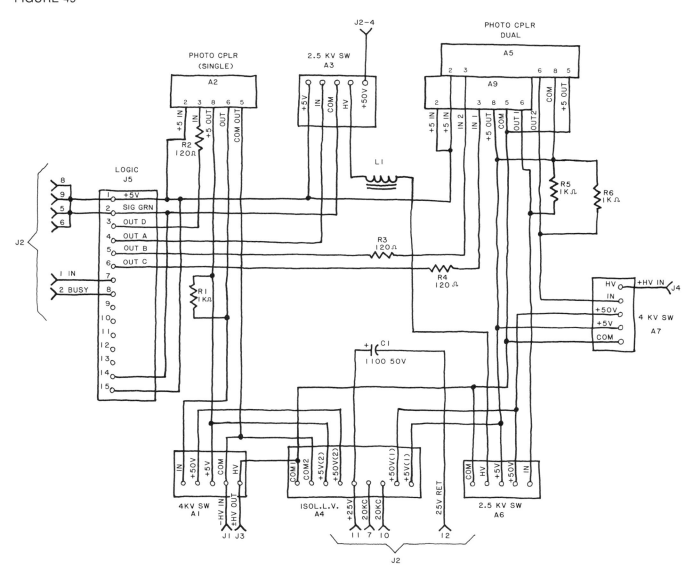

Plate 44. Draw the KEY SWITCH WIRING diagram
sketched in Figure 50.

FIGURE 50

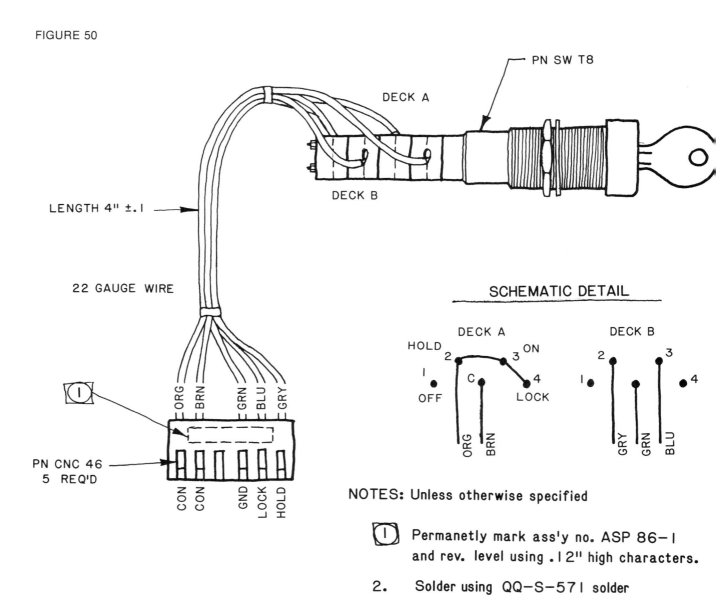

NOTES: Unless otherwise specified

1. Permanetly mark ass'y no. ASP 86-1
and rev. level using .12" high characters.

2. Solder using QQ-S-571 solder

Plate 45. Draw the FLAT CABLE shown in Figure 51.

FIGURE 51

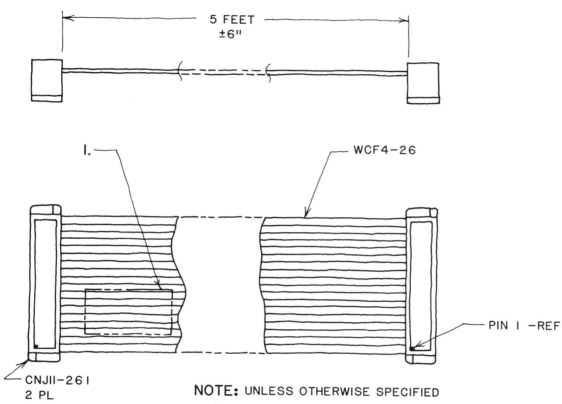

5 FEET
±6"

I.

WCF4−26

PIN I −REF

CNJII−261
2 PL

NOTE: UNLESS OTHERWISE SPECIFIED
I. PLACE ASS'Y NO.,DASH VERSION, AND
REV. LEVEL IN APPROXIMATE AREA SHOWN

48

Plate 46. Complete the INTERFACE CABLE and table shown in Figure 52.

FIGURE 52

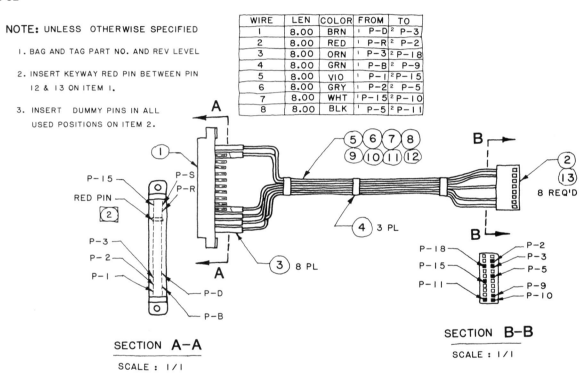

NOTE: UNLESS OTHERWISE SPECIFIED

1. BAG AND TAG PART NO. AND REV LEVEL

2. INSERT KEYWAY RED PIN BETWEEN PIN 12 & 13 ON ITEM 1.

3. INSERT DUMMY PINS IN ALL USED POSITIONS ON ITEM 2.

WIRE	LEN	COLOR	FROM	TO
1	8.00	BRN	¹ P-D	² P-3
2	8.00	RED	¹ P-R	² P-2
3	8.00	ORN	¹ P-3	² P-18
4	8.00	GRN	¹ P-B	² P-9
5	8.00	VIO	¹ P-1	² P-15
6	8.00	GRY	¹ P-2	² P-5
7	8.00	WHT	¹ P-15	² P-10
8	8.00	BLK	¹ P-5	² P-11

SECTION A-A

SCALE : 1/1

SECTION B-B

SCALE : 1/1

Plate 47. Draw the diagram in Figure 53.

FIGURE 53

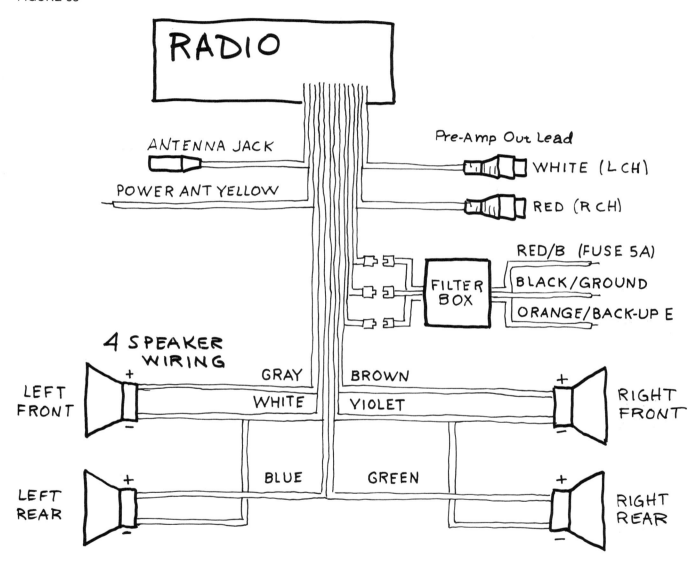

Plate 48. Draw the wiring diagram provided in Figure 54.

FIGURE 54

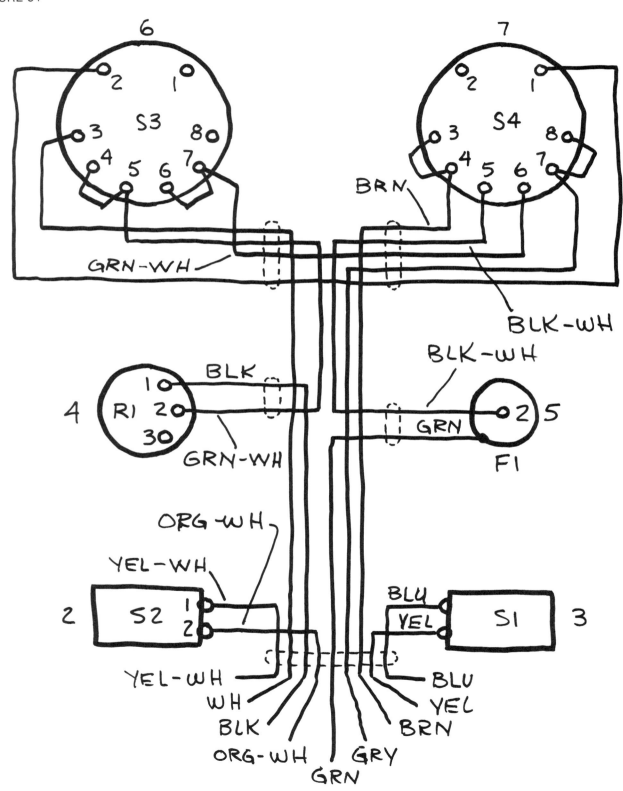

Project 16. Draw the TELEPHONE CIRCUIT shown
in Figure 55.

FIGURE 55

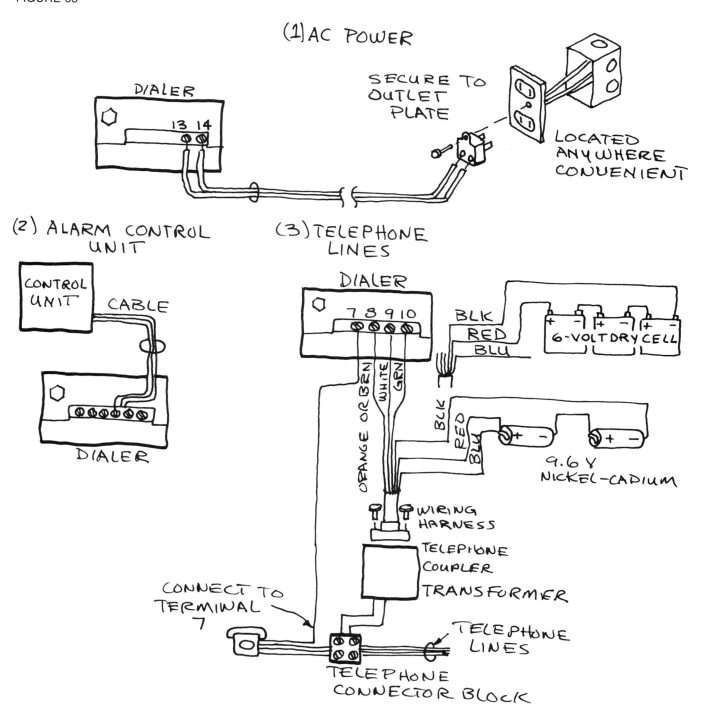

Project 17. Draw the wiring diagram (Figure 56) on a D size sheet.

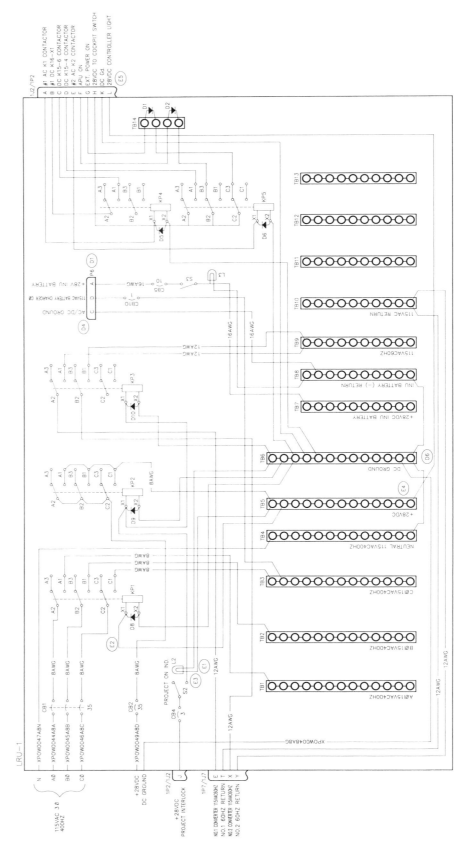

FIGURE 56

Project 18. Draw the FAN AND CONTROL POWER
WIRE ASSEMBLY shown in Figure 57.

FIGURE 57

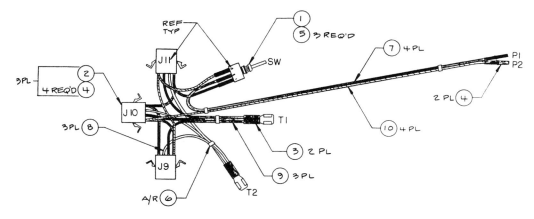

WIRE GA.	COLOR	FROM	TO	LENGTH
20	ORN	SW 1	J11, P1	3.00
	ORN	SW 2	P1	12.00
	ORN	J11, P1	J10, P1	2.50
	ORN	J10, P1	J9, P1	2.50
	WHT	T2	J11, P2	4.50
	WHT	T2	J10, P2	3.50
	WHT	T2	J9, P2	3.00
	BLK	T1	J11, P3	4.00
	BLK	T1	J10, P3	4.00
	BLK	T1	J9, P3	4.00
	GRN	SW3	J11, P4	3.00
	GRN	J11, P4	J9, P4	3.50
	GRN	J9, P4	J10, P4	2.50
20	GRN	J10, P4	P2	12.00

NOTES: UNLESS OTHERWISE SPECIFIED
1. FOR WIRE COLOR & LENGTH
SEE TABLE.
2. BAG & TAG PART NO., DASH VERSION
AND REV LEVEL

	QTY REQD	CODE IDENT	PART OR IDENTIFYING NO.	NOMENCLATURE OR DESCRIPTION			ITEM NO.
	18"		WCW4-205	WIRE, CABLE, GRN. 20GA	4PL	①	10
	18"		WCW4-200	WIRE, CABLE, BLK, 20GA	3PL	①	9
	18"		WCW4-209	WIRE, CABLE, WHT, 20GA	3PL	①	8
	18		WCW4-203	WIRE, CABLE, ORN, 20GA	4PL	①	7
	A/R		WCR1-6	TIE WRAP, PLASTIC, 3/16			6
	3		WCS1-2	SHRINK TUBING, 3/16 DIA X 1/2			5
	14		CNC53	PIN, MOLEX, FEMALE			4
	2		TML5-1	QUICK DISCONNECT LUG			3
	3		CNP85-1	CONNECTOR, MOLEX, 4 PINS			2
	1		SWT2-7103A	SWITCH, TOGGLE			1
-1							

PARTS LIST

UNLESS OTHERWISE SPECIFIED
DIMENSIONS ARE IN INCHES
TOLERANCES ARE:
FRACTIONS   DECIMALS   ANGLES
±   .XX ±.15 ± —
               .XXX ± —

MATERIAL
SEE P/L

FINISH

CONTRACT NO.

APPROVALS   DATE
DRAWN
CHECKED
ENGRG
MFG ENG
QA
APPC

FAN AND CONTROL PWR,
WIRE ASSY

SIZE C   CODE IDENT NO.   DRAWING NO   194-1
REV. A

SCALE FULL   SHEET 1 OF 1

NEXT ASSY   USED ON
APPLICATION   DO NOT SCALE DRAWING

Motors and Control Circuits

(See Chapter 14.)

For most of the assignments in this section, you can use an electrical and electronic ANSI Y32.2 .200 in. grid template. Lettering should be 5/32 in. (4 mm). Space the diagrams to make maximum use of available space. Note that there is little standardization of symbols on air conditioning, refrigeration, and heating manufacturer's wiring and control diagrams. Therefore, an identical circuit drawn by two manufacturers of air conditioning equipment may use a variety of different symbols for the same electrical components. Some major manufacturers may even use two different

symbols for the same component on the same diagram. This lack of standardization may cause some confusion; but as you become more experienced, new symbols for the same component will not present such a problem. Obviously, the drafter must question the engineer to determine that the engineer's sketch contains symbol continuity. This avoids errors and confusion. Many of the following diagrams contain items and symbols that may not be perfect. Construct the problem using templates where possible. All circuit diagrams were taken from equipment manuals.

Plate 49. Draw the CONTROL CIRCUIT sketched in Figure 58.

FIGURE 58

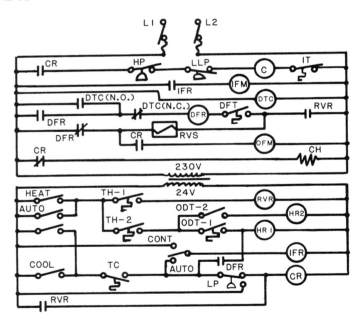

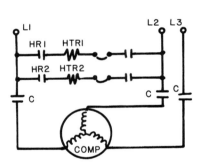

Plate 50. Lay out the THERMOSTAT CONTROL
CIRCUIT shown in Figure 59.

FIGURE 59

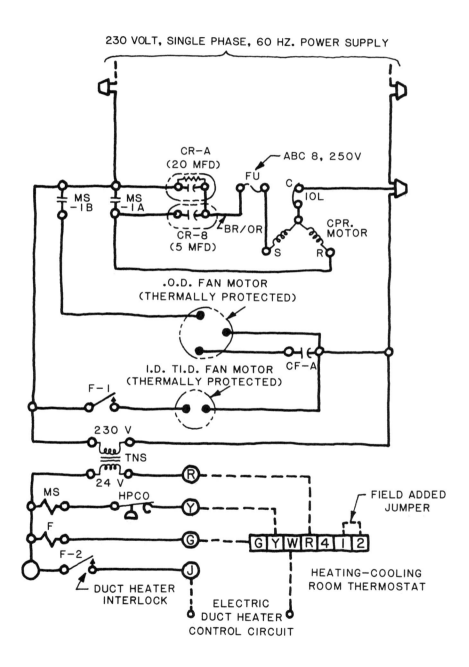

Plate 51. Draw the CONTROL WIRING DIAGRAM shown in Figure 60 using ⅛ in. (3 mm) lettering.

FIGURE 60

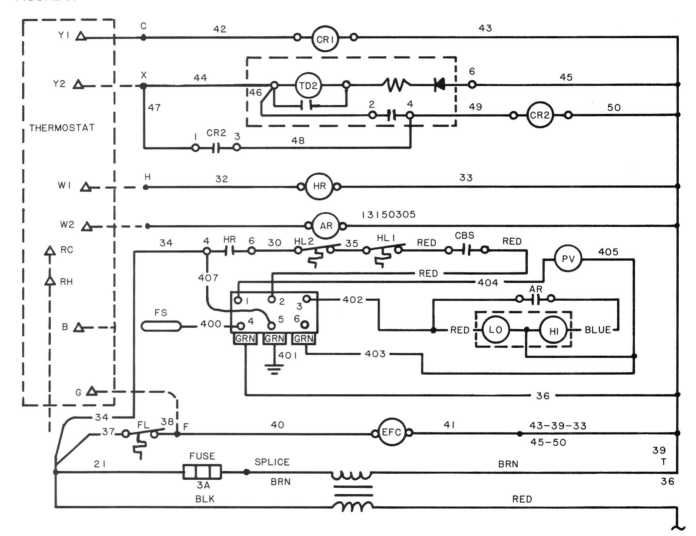

Plate 52. Draw the HEAT PUMP CONTROL CIR-
CUIT sketched in Figure 61.

FIGURE 61

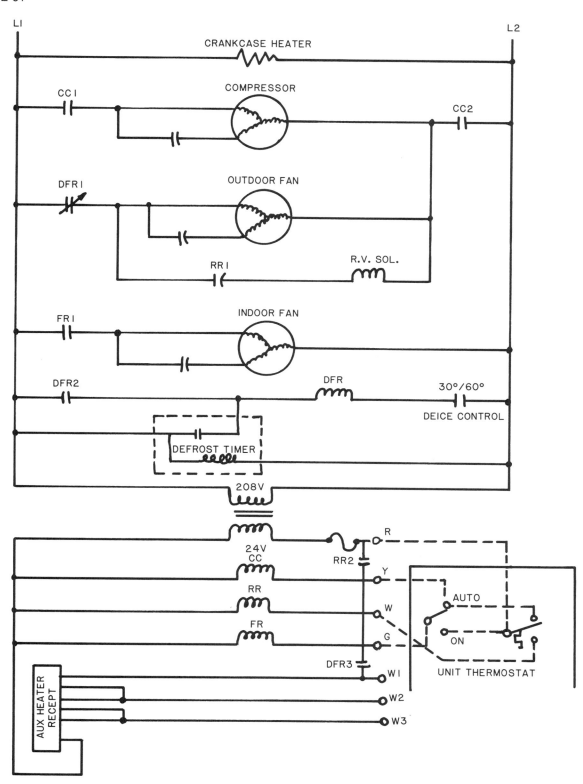

Plate 53. Draw the CONTROL CIRCUIT in Figure 62.

FIGURE 62

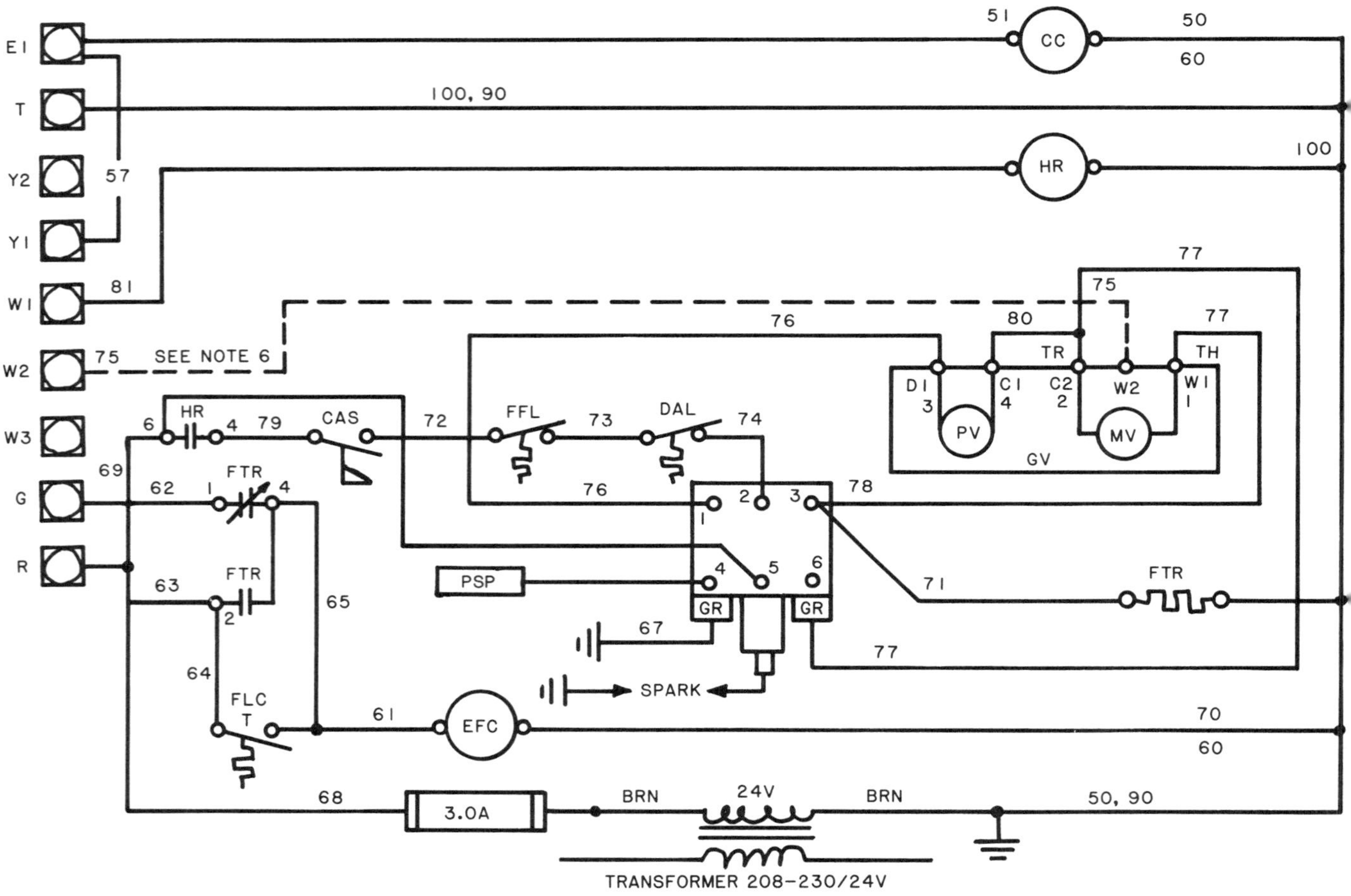

Plate 54. Draw the wiring diagram for the furnace-air conditioner unit shown in Figure 63.

FIGURE 63

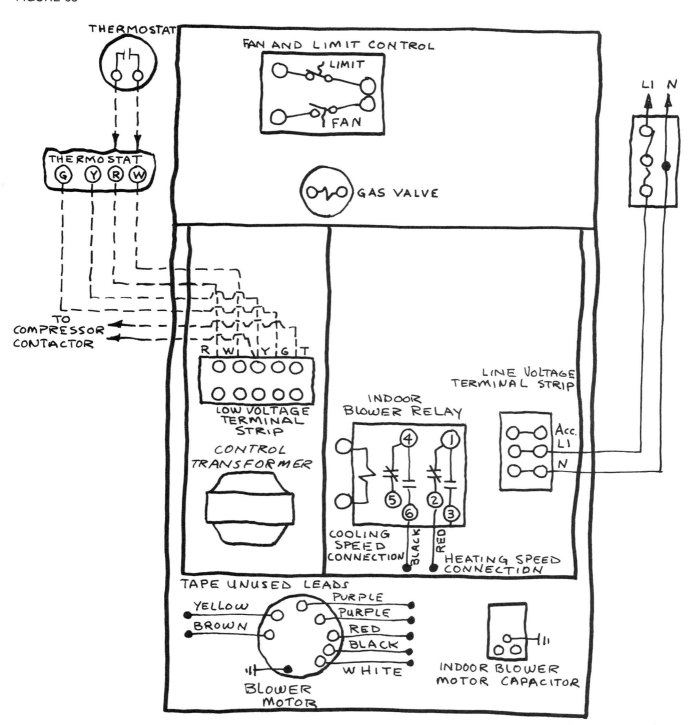

60

Project 19. Draw the POWER SUPPLY shown in Figure 64 on a C size sheet.

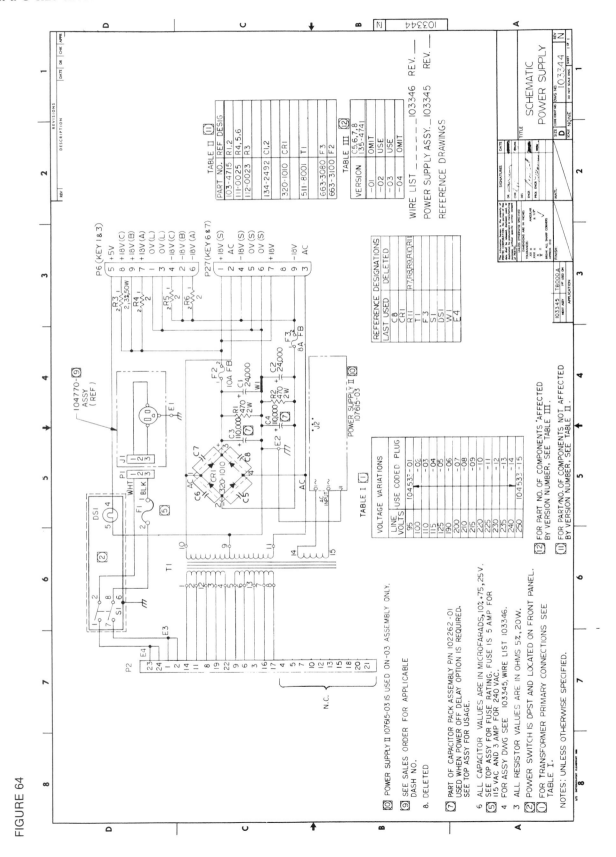

FIGURE 64

Project 20. Draw the POWER SEQUENCING CONTROL circuit (Figure 65).

FIGURE 65

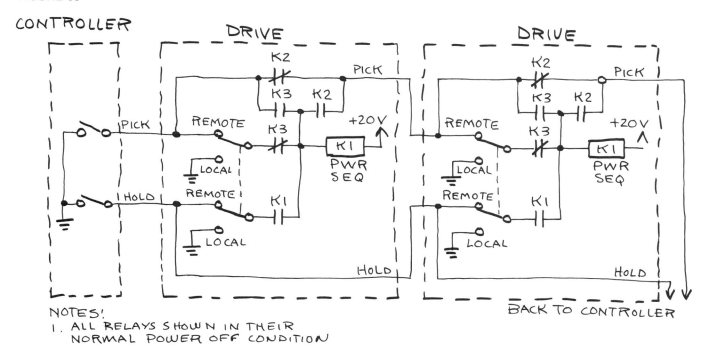

NOTES!
1. ALL RELAYS SHOWN IN THEIR NORMAL POWER OFF CONDITION

Project 21. Draw the POWER ON circuit (Figure 66) on a C size sheet.

FIGURE 66

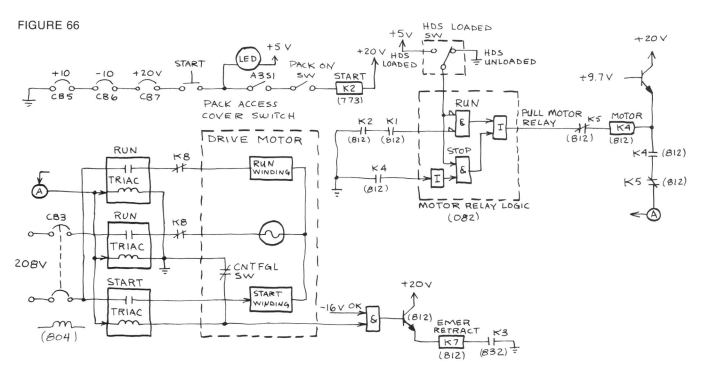

Project 22. Draw the EMERGENCY RETRACT circuit shown in Figure 67.

FIGURE 67

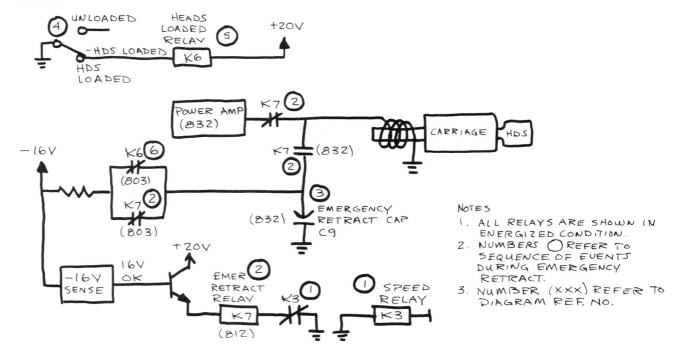

Project 23. Draw the FEEDBACK CONTROL circuit shown in Figure 68.

FIGURE 68

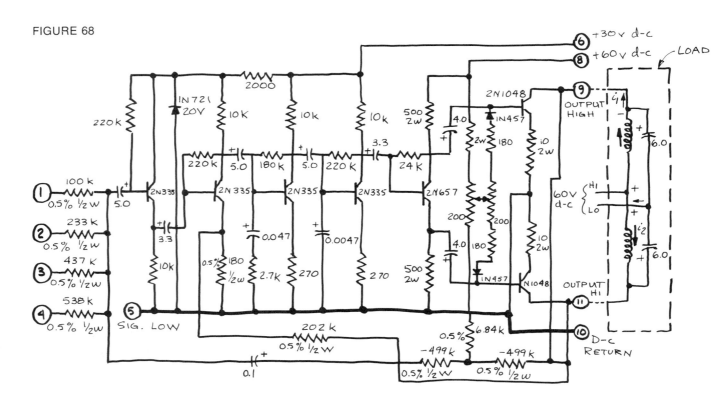

Programmable Controllers and Robotics

(See Chapter 15.)

Draw the following problems using the same general instructions as for Chapter 14.

Plate 55. Draw the graph of the PERFORMANCE ANALYSIS OF THE FEEDBACK CONTROL SYSTEM shown in Figure 69.

FIGURE 69

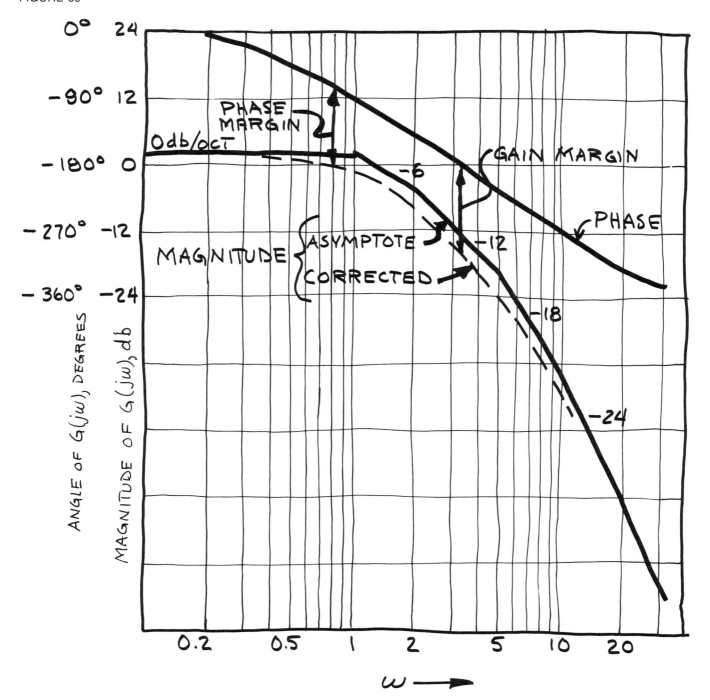

Plate 56. Draw the graph of the RELAY SERVO
CONTROL SYSTEM provided in Figure 70.

FIGURE 70

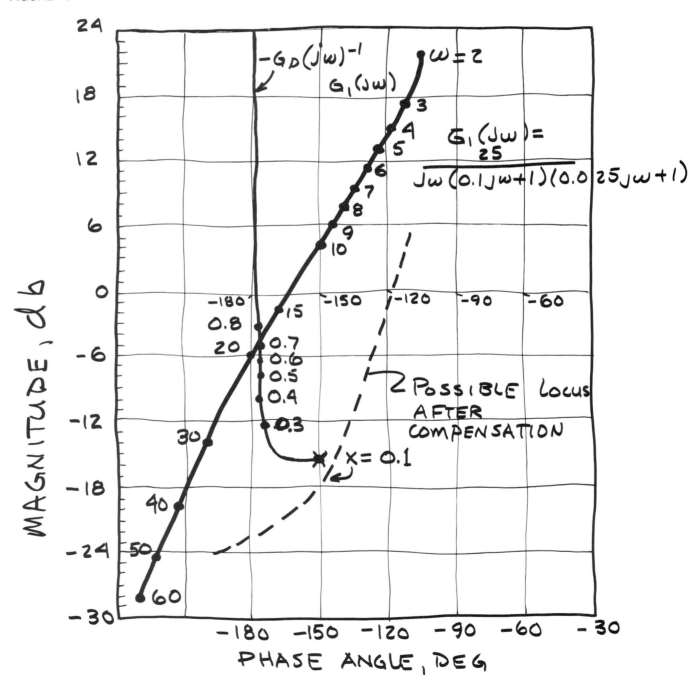

Plate 57. Draw the diagram for the MODEL-BASED MANIPULATOR CONTROL SYSTEM for a robot shown in Figure 71.

FIGURE 71

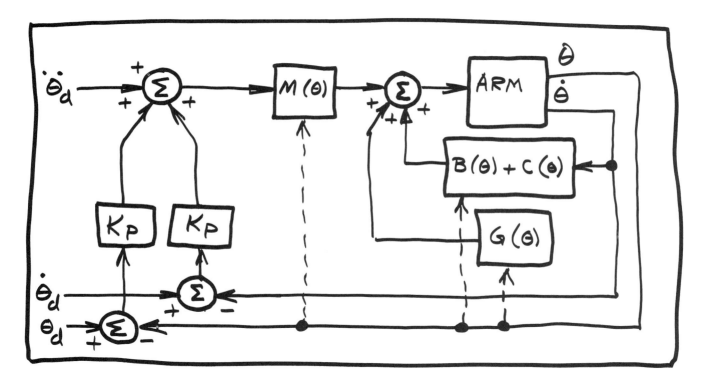

Plate 58. Draw the diagram for the FORCE CON-
TROLLER OF THE ROBOT MANIPULATOR given
in Figure 72.

FIGURE 72

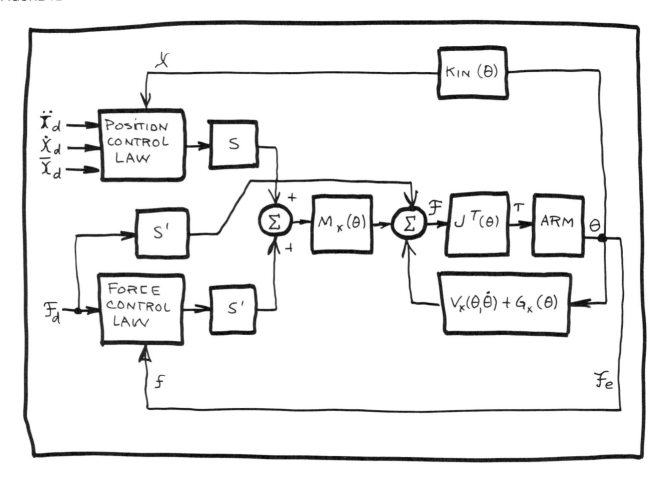

Plate 59. Draw the SERVO AMPLIFIER for the robot shown in Figure 73.

FIGURE 73

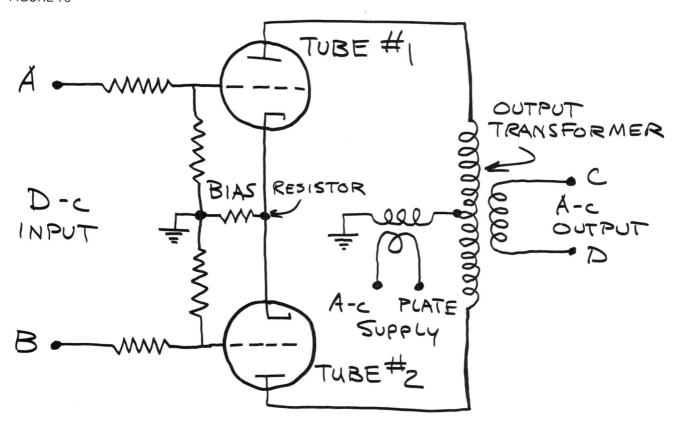

Plate 60. Draw the ROBOT RELAY CONTROLLER
shown in Figure 74.

FIGURE 74

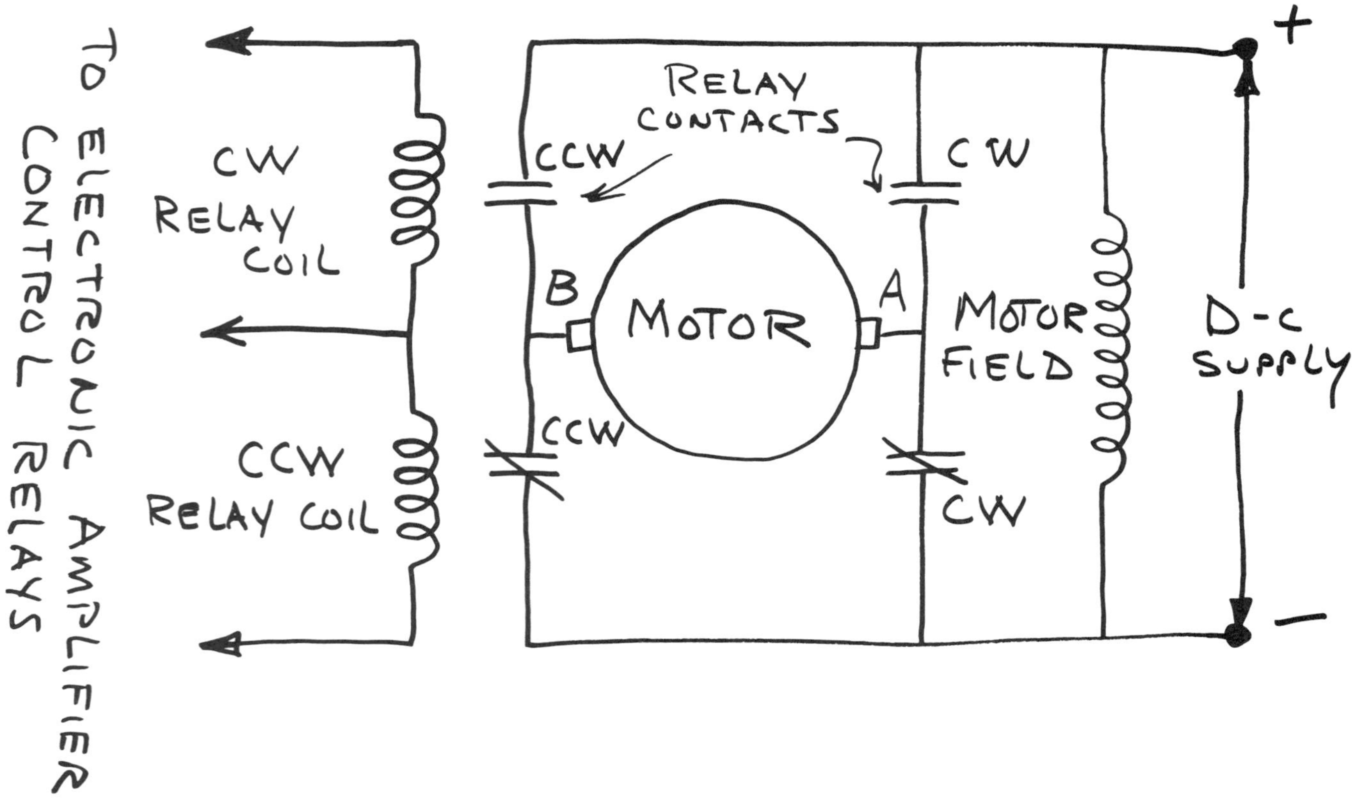

Project 24. Draw the diagram of the SERVO ROBOT shown in Figure 75 on a C size sheet.

FIGURE 75

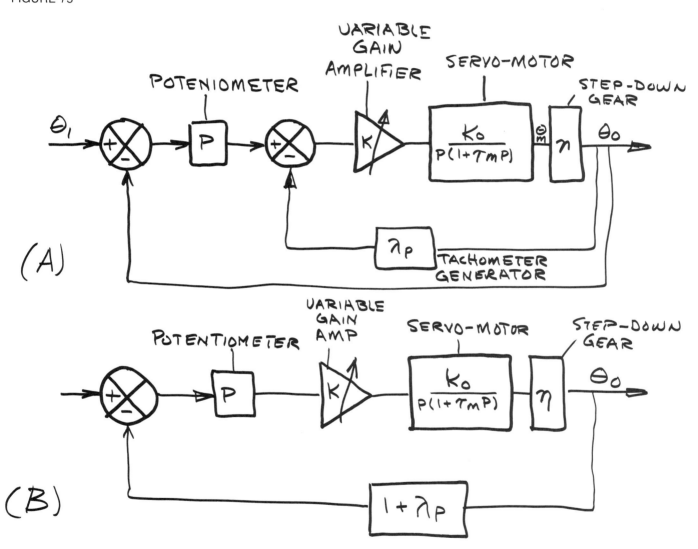

Project 25. Draw the diagram of the ROBOT INDUC-
TION CONTROL MOTOR provided in Figure 76.

FIGURE 76

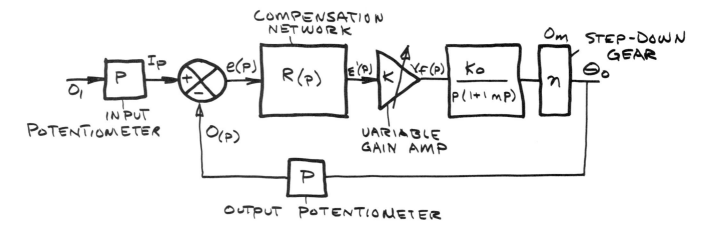

Project 26. Draw the ROBOT CONTROL SYSTEM
shown in Figure 77 on a B size sheet.

FIGURE 77

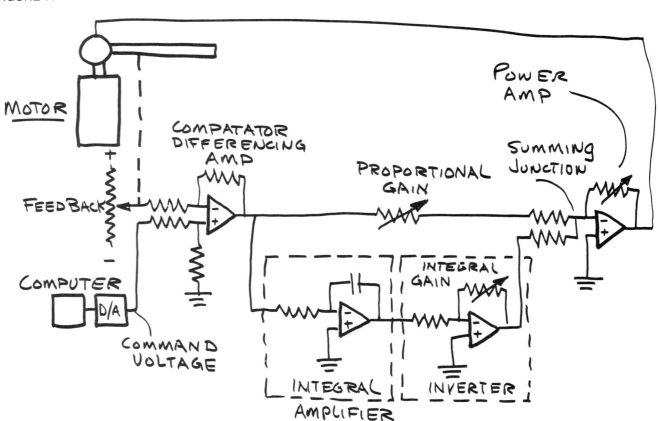

Power Distribution

(See Chapter 16.)

Use specifications provided in Chapter 16 and the appendices to complete the following plates and projects.

Plate 61. Draw the FOUR-WIRE PANEL CONNECTION given in Figure 78.

FIGURE 78

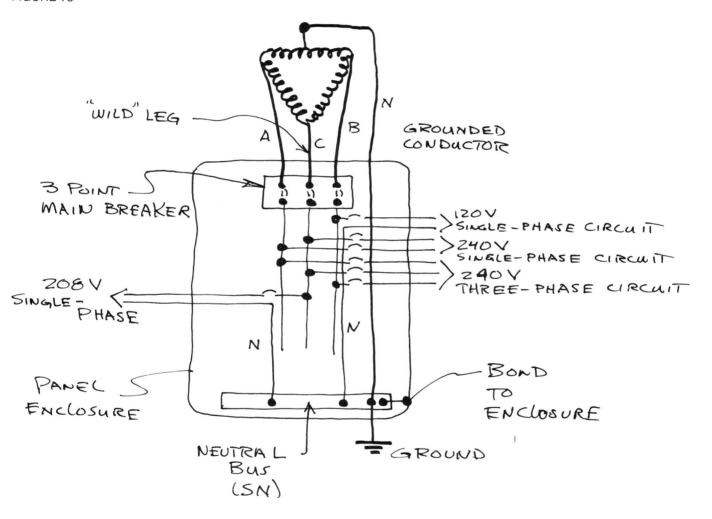

Plate 62. Draw the MAIN BREAKER AND PANEL
circuit shown in Figure 79.

FIGURE 79

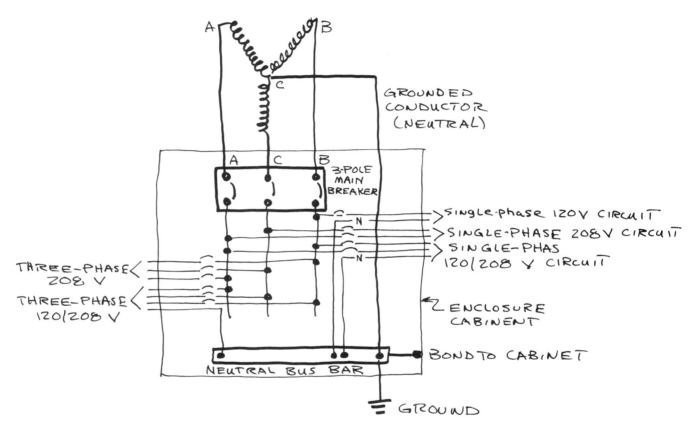

Plate 63. Draw the MOTOR ELECTRICAL schematic
shown in Figure 80.

FIGURE 80

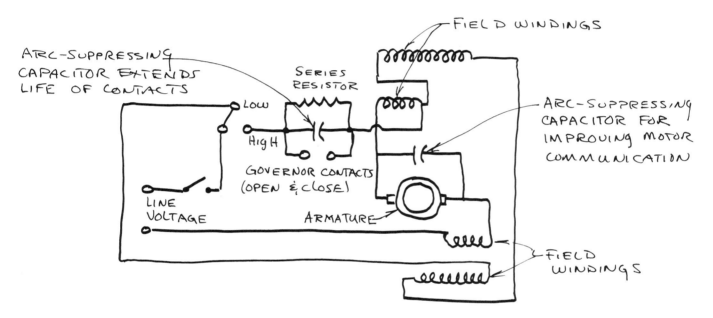

Plate 64. Draw the ARMSTRONG OSCILLATOR circuit provided in Figure 81.

FIGURE 81

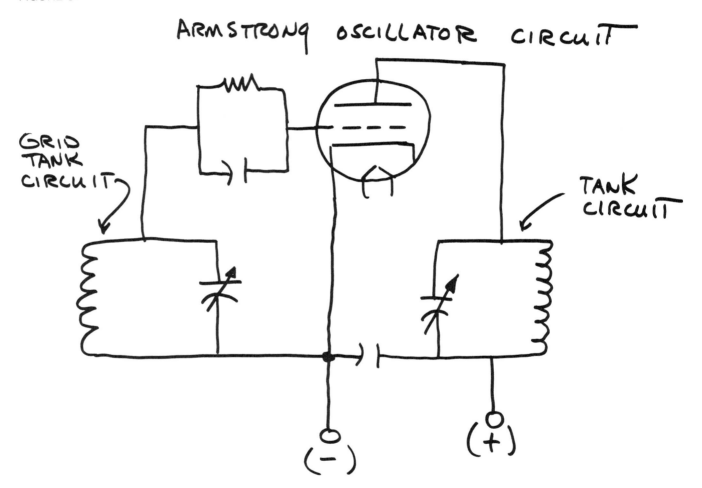

Plate 65. Draw the INSTANT-ON SWITCH given in Figure 82.

FIGURE 82

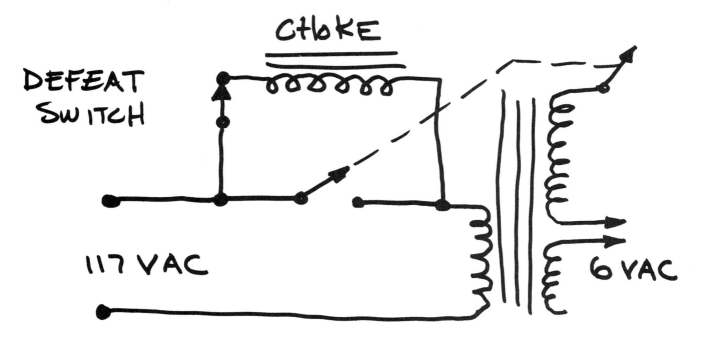

INSTANT-ON SWITCH

CHOKE

DEFEAT SWITCH

117 VAC

6 VAC

76

Plate 66. Draw the DC MOTOR shown in Figure 83.

FIGURE 83

SHUNT
MOTOR

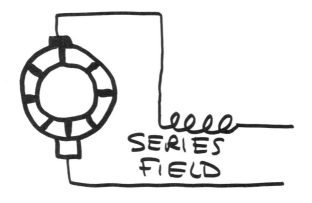

SERIES
MOTOR

COMPOUND
MOTOR

Project 27. Draw the DUAL VOLTAGE COMMER-
CIAL POOL circuit given in Figure 84.

FIGURE 84

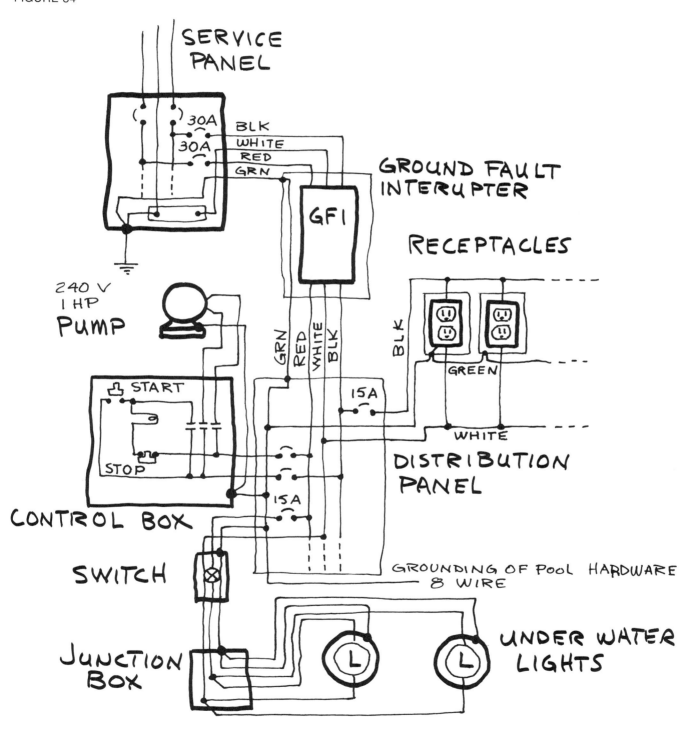

Project 28. Draw the POWER circuit shown in Figure 85.

FIGURE 85

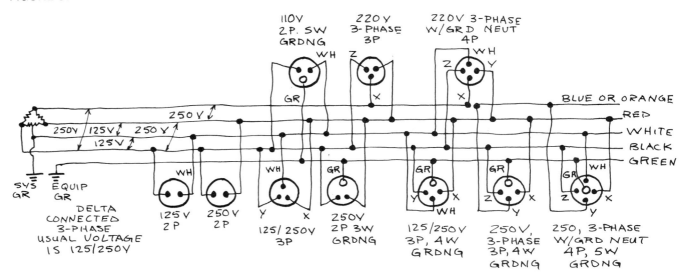

Project 29. Draw the pole transformer hook-up 3X book size (Figure 86).

FIGURE 86

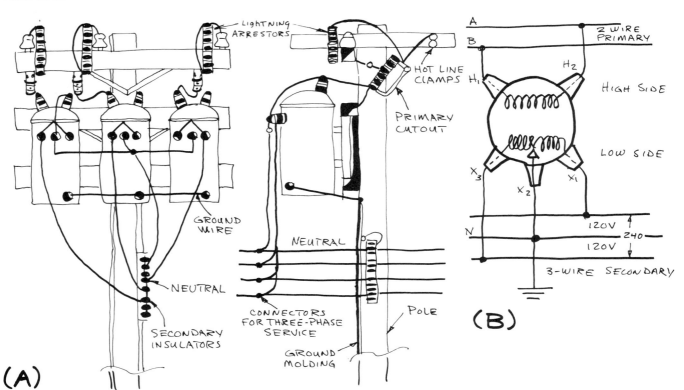

Electronic Packaging

(See Chapter 17.)

Consult Chapter 3 for lettering standards, Chapter 5 for dimensioning conventions, and Chapter 6 for information on pictorial projections while completing this section.

Plate 67. Using Figure 87, dimension the CONNECTOR using the datum-line dimensioning method. The 0–0 position will be in the lower left corner. Use dimension lines only for the outline of the part.

For hole callouts, use a hole location chart. Give the hole size/description, quantity, and the X and Y dimension location. All holes are through the piece.

Plate 68. Dimension the PANEL using coordinate dimensioning without dimension lines. Establish the 0–0 position in the lower right corner for datum reference. Locate all holes and the object's outline on the drawing. On a separate sheet construct a hole description table with the hole identifying letter, description, and quantity. Letter the holes starting from the smallest size as "A."

Plate 69. Complete the right side view of the POLARIZER BRACKET and dimension using the coordinate dimensioning method without dimension lines. Position 0–0 of the base/datum lines will have its origin at the lower right corner of the piece. All holes are through the piece.

FIGURE 87

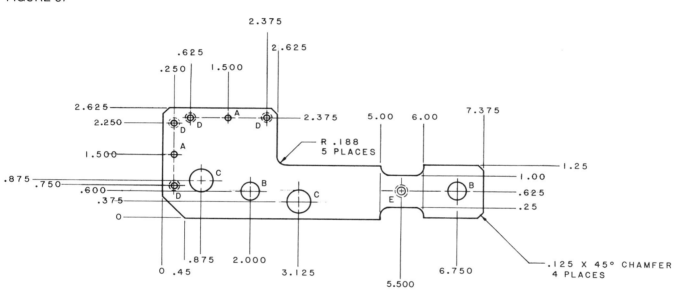

.25 ALY ALUM ANODIZE BLACK

HOLE	DESCRIPTION	QTY
A	Ø .125 THRU	2
B	Ø .375 THRU	2
C	Ø .50 THRU	2
D	Ø .149 THRU Ø .281 X .073 DP FS	4
E	8-32 UNC-2B	1

Plate 70. Using Figure 88 of the HOLD DOWN, construct an isometric view of the piece. Do not dimension. Note that Figure 88 shows a flat pattern development of the sheet metal part. Place the front left corner in the given starting point on the plate.

FIGURE 88

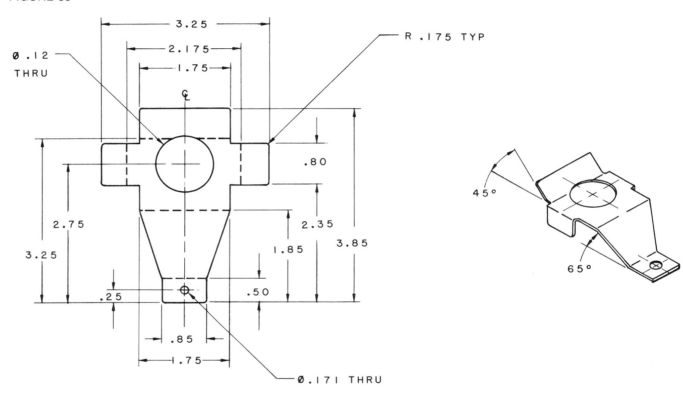

NOTES:

1. DASHED LINES ARE BEND LINES

.BERYLLIUM COPPER.020 THK

Plate 71. Draw and dimension the SPRING JIG shown
in Figure 89. Show the left side and the auxiliary view
of the piece. Do not use the datum-line method.

FIGURE 89

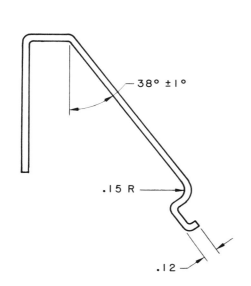

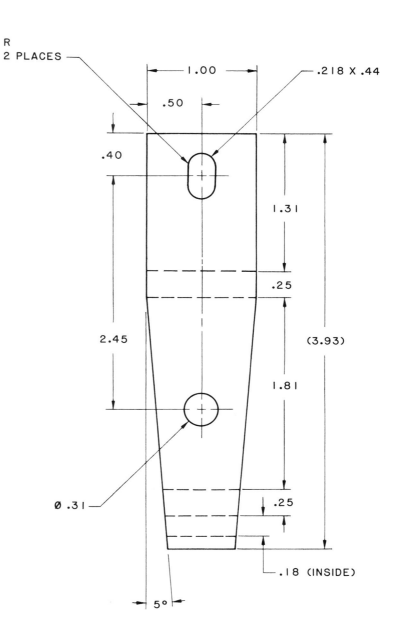

NOTES:

1. USE .010/.020 BEND RADIUS
   EXCEPT WHERE NOTED

2. ALL BENDS TO BE 90°
   EXCEPT WHERE NOTED

3. AFTER FABRICATION HEAT
   TREAT TO CONDITION 1050

Plate 72. Draw the CRT HOLDER shown in Figure 90. Show the part in oblique projection, but do not dimension. Instructor may assign this project to be developed into a flat pattern on a B size sheet for extra credit.

FIGURE 90

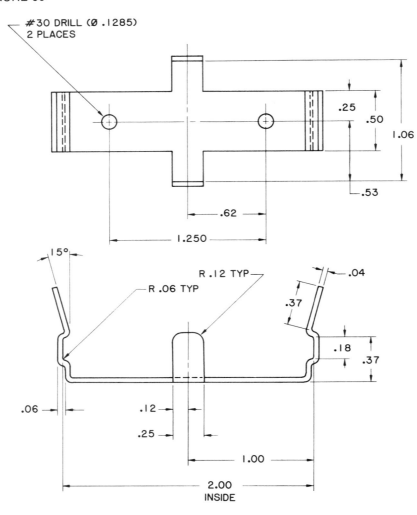

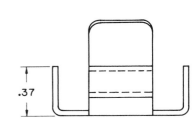

NOTES:

1. HEAT TREAT TO CONDITION R.H. 950
   (REF. JORGENSEN STEEL BOOK)
   HEAT CONDITION "A" MATERIAL
   TO 1750° F FOR 10 MIN. COOL TO 100° F AND HOLD FOR 8 HOURS
   HEAT TO 950° F AND HOLD FOR 1 HOUR. COOL IN AIR TO ROOM TEMP.

Project 30. Using Figure 91, develop the SUBPANEL and dimension completely. Use a hole chart. Draw the project on a C size sheet.

FIGURE 91

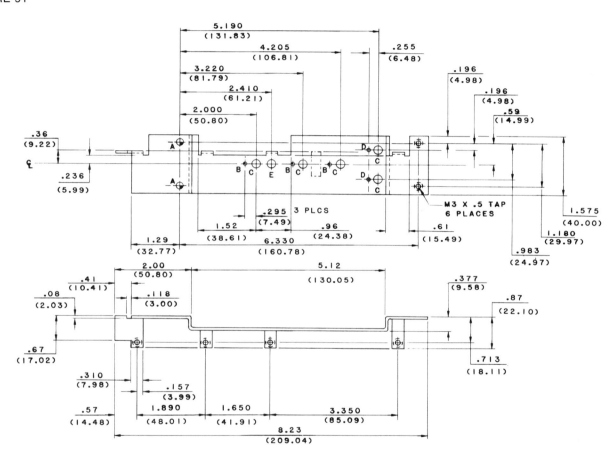

NOTES:

1. REMOVE ALL BURRS AND SHARP EDGES

2. BEND RADII .06 MAX

3. MARK PART NO. NEARSIDE

HOLE CHART		
CODE	DESCRIPTION±.005	QTY
A	.140 (3.56)	2
B	1.109 (2.78)	3
C	.219 (5.56)	5
D	.094 (2.38)	2
E	.188 (4.76)	1

Project 31. Redraw the ELECTRONIC UNIT BRACKET shown in Figure 92 on a C size sheet and dimension as shown. Draw a full-scale isometric on a B size sheet. The third part of this project involves constructing a flat pattern development without dimensions.

FIGURE 92

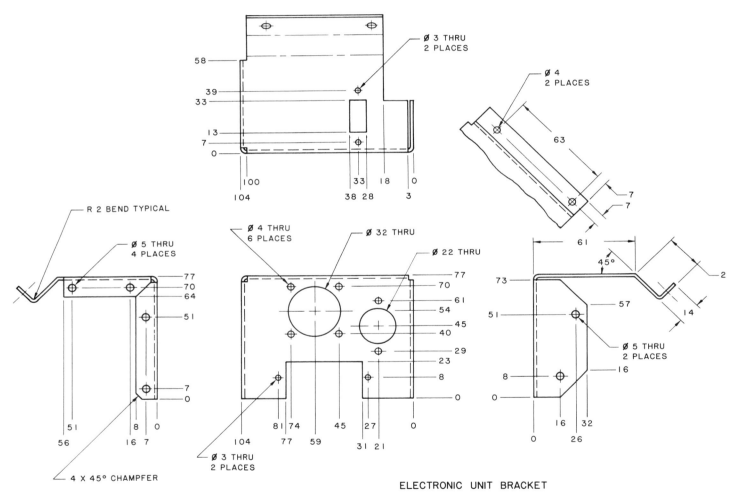

ELECTRONIC UNIT BRACKET

Project 32. Draw the FRONT PANEL on a C size sheet (Figure 93). Also lay out a flat pattern development of the part on a separate C size sheet. Dimension completely.

FIGURE 93

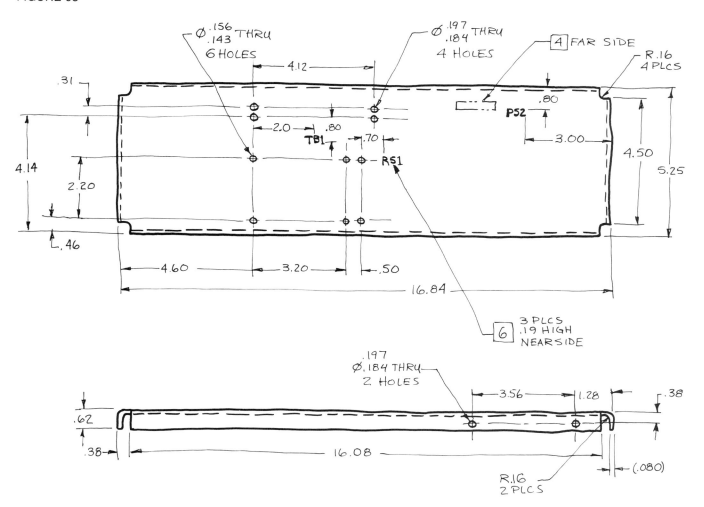

86

Project 33. Draw the PANEL and dimension completely (Figure 94).

FIGURE 94

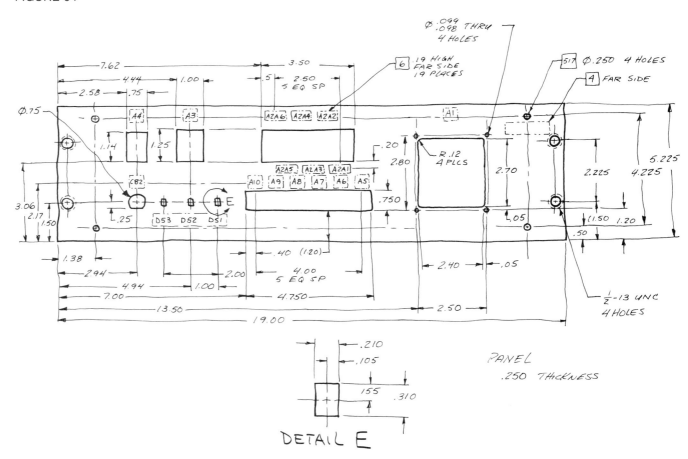

DETAIL E

GENERAL PRINTED CIRCUIT BOARD INSTRUCTIONS

Printed Circuit Boards

(See Chapter 18.)

Lay out the PCB represented by the diagrams shown in sections covering LOGIC DIAGRAMS and SCHEMATIC DIAGRAMS. The board geometry has been

provided for each PCB assignment in this section. For each of the boards to be designed, use the following specifications:

A. Scale: 2:1.
B. Medium: 10 × 10 grid (nonreproducible). A 10 × 10 grid underlay is provided at the end of the workbook.
C. Color code: component side traces blue and solder side traces red.

D. Trace widths: signal lines—.015 in. wide, power/ ground lines and primary bus—.100 in. wide, secondary bus lines—.050 in. wide.
E. Pad diameters: .050, .062, .100, .150, .200 and .250 in. at 2:1 scale.
F. Component placement: all on 10 × 10 grid cross hairs.
G. Feedthru pads: .050 in.
H. Power pins or Vcc: normally pins 1 and 31 for most digital PCBs, but instructor may wish to change the pin assignments.
I. Ground pins or Vdd: normally pins 30 and 60 for most digital boards, but assignments can be changed.
J. Put three registration targets, reduction marks, and reduction size (at ±.005 in. tolerance) on all analog boards where this information is not given.

ARTWORK TAPE-UP MASTER RULES

1. Use the *pad master* as shown in Figure 95. Using prepunch .003, .005, or .007 clear film, align the film with registration pins. The film will be laid on top of the red and blue layout drawing. If registration pins and prepunched film are not available, then use registration targets and register each layer of film to the layout. Place the correct size pads as required for the pad master.

2. *Registration:* all pads will be centered on the grid cross hairs. Apply reduction marks and dimensions as required. All reduction dimensions will have a ±.005 in. tolerance. Place three registration marks outside the board outline.

FIGURE 95

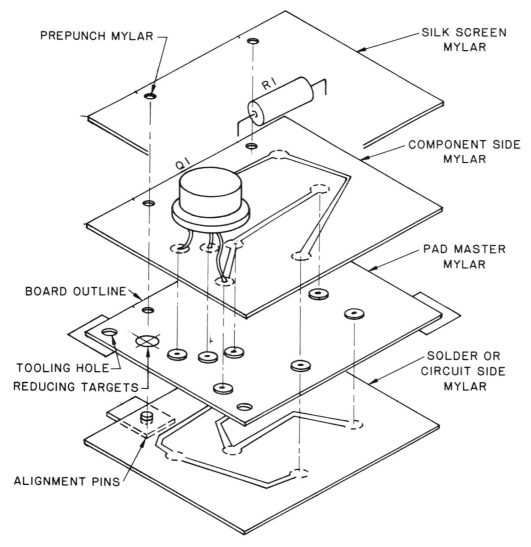

PREPUNCH MYLAR
SILK SCREEN MYLAR
R1
COMPONENT SIDE MYLAR
Q1
PAD MASTER MYLAR
BOARD OUTLINE
TOOLING HOLE
REDUCING TARGETS
SOLDER OR CIRCUIT SIDE MYLAR
ALIGNMENT PINS

Tape—up

3. *Pad master overlay* (Figure 95): put three tooling
holes on each board when they are not already provided. For the following components, use a square
pad (Figure 96): (a) transistor emitters; (b) pin 1 and
all DIP packages (unless the given layout marks pin
1 with a dot or a different shape pad); (c) capacitors
that are polarized (square pad for the plus side); (d)
cathode end for diodes; (e) wiper side for variable
resistors; (f) pin 1 on SIPS resistor packs; and (g)
jumper wires. Note that the pad master will have
the board geometry shown on it. Use preprinted
pads if available.

FIGURE 96

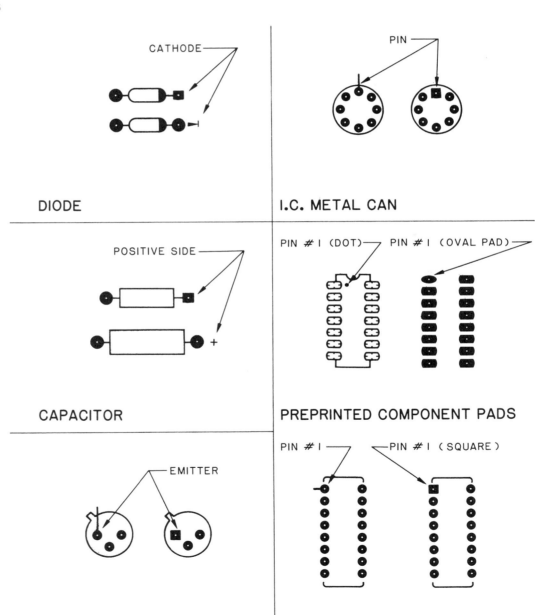

DIODE

I.C. METAL CAN

CAPACITOR

PREPRINTED COMPONENT PADS

TRANSISTOR

I.C. DUAL IN LINE

4. *Solder side* (Figure 97): This is the next overlay that will be placed on or under the pad master. Show all red traces on this overlay. Show the following on this layout: SOLDER SIDE in large letters, board part number, board revision letter, and serial number. These will normally be shown on this document but reversed. Use tape for conductor traces when available.

5. *Component side* (Figure 97): This is the next overlay that will be placed over the pad master. Show all blue traces that are on the layout. Show COMPONENT SIDE in large lettering on this document along with the assembly number of the board, if provided. Use tape when available.

6. *Silkscreen* (Figure 95): This will be the last overlay to be placed on the pad master. It will show the location of all components and reference designations. Use template or Leroy lettering. Ink the drawing unless instructor requests otherwise. Pre-printed component outlines may also be used.

FIGURE 97

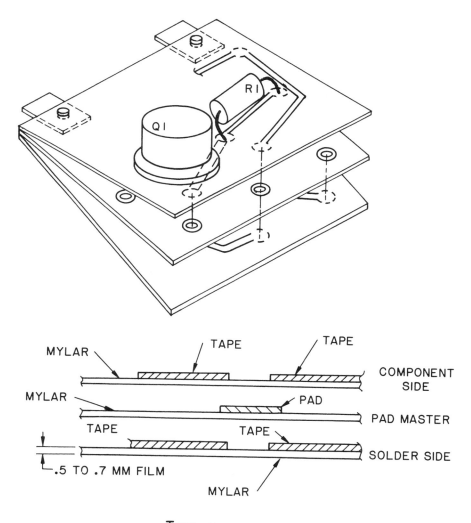

Tape—up

BOARD FABRICATION RULES

1. A board fabrication drawing shows the board geometry, dimensions, and tolerances (Figure 98).
2. Note the board material, G10, G10-FR or another material.
3. A table showing hole diameters, tolerance, and number of holes should be included on the drawing. Code the holes so that they can be identified on the circuit side of the board.
4. Include the name, number, and any other specifications that may apply to the part.
5. The circuit side pattern images should be shown with all traces and pads. Holes are drilled from the circuit side of the board.
6. If the board is multilayer, each layer should be indicated on a cross-section view of the board with thickness and tolerance given.

FIGURE 98

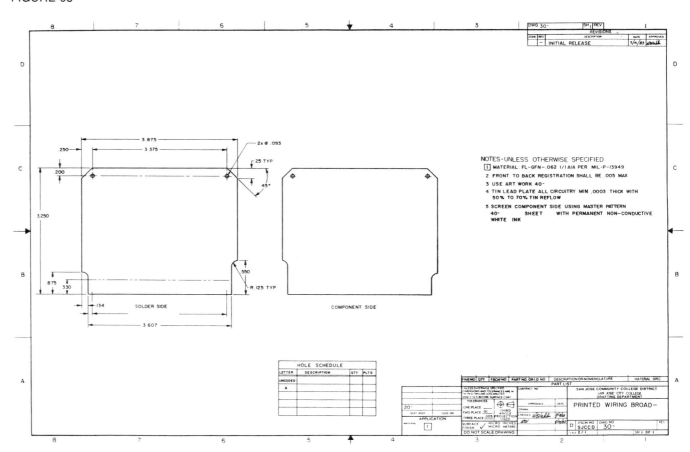

ASSEMBLY DRAWING RULES

1. The assembly drawing should show component placement and reference designation markings, assembly specifications, and test specifications. Include a list of materials to be ordered.
2. The assembly drawing is viewed from the component side of the board.
3. Orientation and indexing of all transistor tabs, polarized capacitors, diodes, variable resistors, DIP packages, connector pin 1, and every tenth pin should be indicated.
4. All specifications should be included in the notes on this drawing (see Figure 99).

FIGURE 99

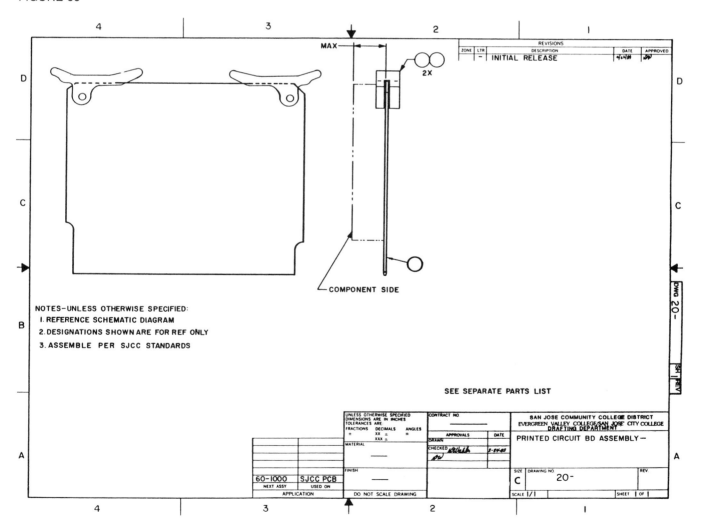

PARTS LIST RULES

The term *parts list* applies to a tabulation of parts and materials required to fabricate or produce the end item shown on the drawing: PCB, mechanical part, or panel assembly, for examples. Four parts lists are provided at the end of the workbook. Photocopy the list if more than four are needed to complete the assignments.

Parts List Entries

1. Company or school name, address, and/or logo.
2. Person's name who prepared the drawing.
3. Person's name who checked the drawing.
4. The engineer responsible for the project.
5. Revision letter of the latest change to the document.
6. Drawing or document number applicable to the material or type designation as assigned by the school or company.
7. The description or nomenclature that describes the items whose part or identifying number appears in column 6.
8. Manufacturing number, the part number assigned by the vendor from which your company will purchase the item.
9. Quantity required denoting the exact number/amount of each piece required to complete a single item shown on the drawing.
10. Reference designation or specification. On electronics drawings, the reference designation for parts is required (for example, R1, C1, Q10, CR5, T6). On mechanical drawings or for mechanical parts, the material specification should be called out (for example, AL Aly 5052-H32).
11. Item numbers that are used to balloon or call out separate pieces (parts) and must be included on the parts list.
12. Sheet list to establish the sheet number and the total sheet count of a project (for example, sheet 3 of 6, sheet 2 of 8).

PCB PROBLEMS

Lay out the following printed circuit assignments following the instructions previously provided.

Analog PC Design

Plate 73. HIGH-SPEED ANALOG COMPARATOR. Use the schematic diagram in Figure 1 to lay out the board.

Plate 74. DUAL SCHMITT TRIGGERS. Use the schematic diagram in Figure 2.

Plate 75. BUFFER AMPLIFIER (complete design package documentation). Use the schematic diagram in Figure 3. Complete the parts list using the form sheets at the end of the workbook.

Plate 76. 2 KV NEGATIVE POWER SUPPLY. Use the schematic diagram in Figure 7.

Digital PC Design

Plate 77. FLASHER CIRCUIT. Use the diagram from Figure 38.

Plate 78. INPUT NAND GATES–DTL. Use the logic diagram from Figure 34.

Plate 79. INPUT CAPACITY DRIVER NAND GATES–DTL. Use the logic diagram from Figure 35.

Plate 80. SIX FORM "A" REED RELAYS WITH 3-INPUT DRIVERS–DTL (complete design package documentation). Use the logic diagram from Figure 36. Complete the parts list using the forms provided at the end of the workbook.

Plate 81. TWELVE-BIT SHIFT REGISTER W/ GATED PARALLEL ENTRY–DTL. Use the logic diagram from Figure 37.

Plate 82. CLOCK STORAGE–DTL. Use the diagram from Figure 39.

SURFACE-MOUNTED DEVICE DESIGN

In the early 1980s a significant trend developed toward the use of surface-mounted devices (SMDs). Surface-mounted devices replaced dual in-line packages (DIPs) and other thru-hole mounting devices in new printed circuit board designs for a variety of applications.

The benefits of using SMDs include a 30–60% down-sizing of boards, a reduction in weight, and lower production costs. Increased assembly speed is also attained when robots are used for production. Other benefits are improved reliability and test results. When SMDs are utilized, components can be placed closer and on both sides of the board. Also, improved reaction to shock, vibration, and thermal management can be attained.

The primary advantage of SMDs over DIPs in achieving high circuit packing density is smaller component size—typically an SMD is 25% smaller than for a comparable DIP. In addition, since holes in the board are not required for mounting SMDs, these packages can be mounted without regard to electrical shorting between coincident packages. Because fewer holes have to be drilled in fabricating boards which use SMDs, the final board may cost less and typically is easier to manufacture.

Surface-Mounted Printed Circuit Boards

One of the major factors that has encouraged the utilization of surface-mount technology in system design is the use of CAD. CAD can accommodate the design rule changes which must be applied. The areas that have been developed by CAD vendors fall into four basic categories: database structure, system flexibility, component placement and routing, and manufacturing support.

As in any other PCB design, the designer needs the following information: schematic or logic diagram, artwork ceramic substrate size and routing, and manufacturing information.

From the receipt of the circuit diagram, a layout conforming to the basic design rules takes into account the customer's packaging specifications, dissipation limits, interconnections, etc. A CAD system can originate a multilayer board and generate the required art-work to form masks for production of the surface-mount design.

In order to start an SMD board, the same information is required as for a standard discrete component board. (See the previously listed general printed circuit board instructions, the artwork tape-up master rules, the board fabrication rules, and the assembly drawing rules.) The serial/parallel port PCB shown in Figure 100 (A thru J) is an example of a two-sided board using SMDs in its design. If a multisided board was required, the new circuit trace layers would be added. The documentation required for an SMD board is given as follows:

1. Logic diagram (Figure 100 (A)).
2. Padmaster for gang hole drilling on a CNC machine (Figure 100 (B)).
3. Padmaster for component side with component pads and circuit traces (Figure 100 (C)).
4. Padmaster solder side with circuit traces and component pads or feed-thru (Figure 100 (D)).
5. Masktop component pads and feed-thrus (Figure 100 (E)).
6. Maskbottom with feed-thrus (Figure 100 (F)).
7. Silkscreen (painted in white or yellow) (Figure 100 (G)).
8. Pastetop used in assembly and manufacturing of the board (Figure 100 (H)).
9. Assembly drawing (Figure 100 (I)).
10. Fabrication drawing (Figure 100 (J)).

SMD PCB Design

For each of the SMD PCB projects you must design a board. Keep the board geometry as simple as possible. Your instructor may wish to supply the board design. Where required, substitute discrete components called out on the diagram with SMD components. Consult SMD catalogs for appropriate components.

Project 34. Use Figure 10 as the circuit for the board.

Project 35. Use the schematic provided in Figure 12 for the circuit requirements.

Project 36. Use the VERTICAL DEFLECTION CIRCUIT shown in Figure 16 to lay out the board.

FIGURE 100(A)

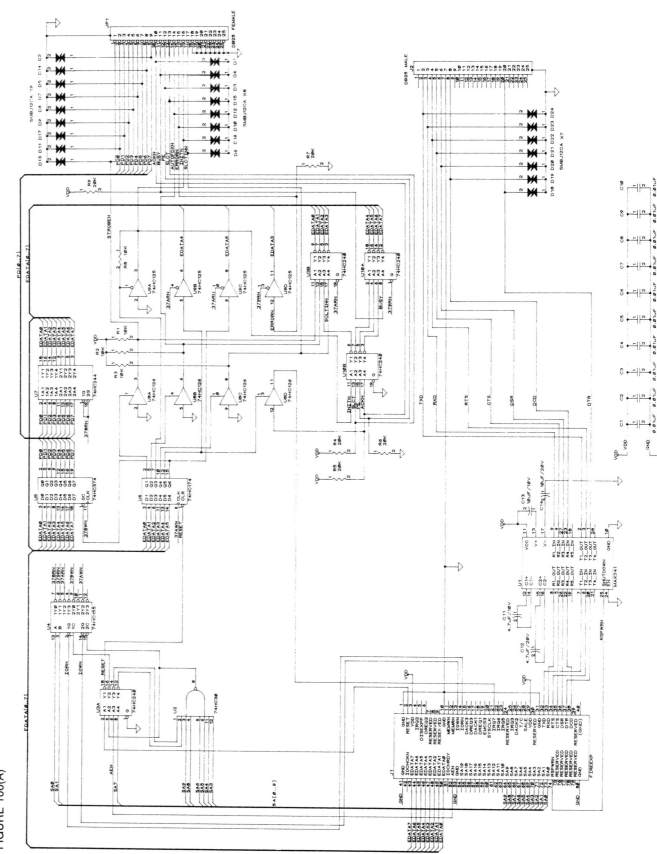

FIGURE 100(B)

FIGURE 100(C)

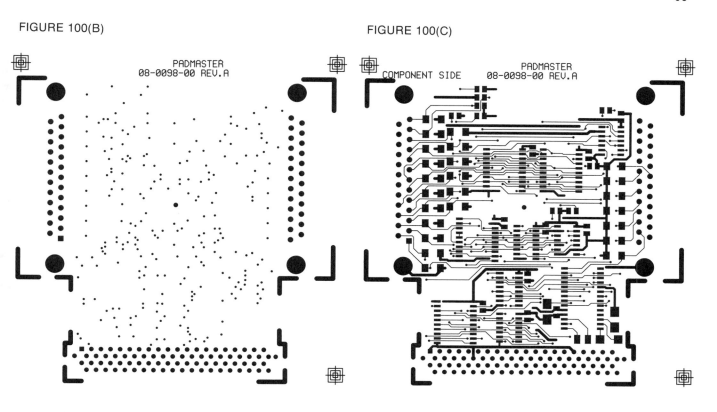

FIGURE 100(D)

FIGURE 100(E)

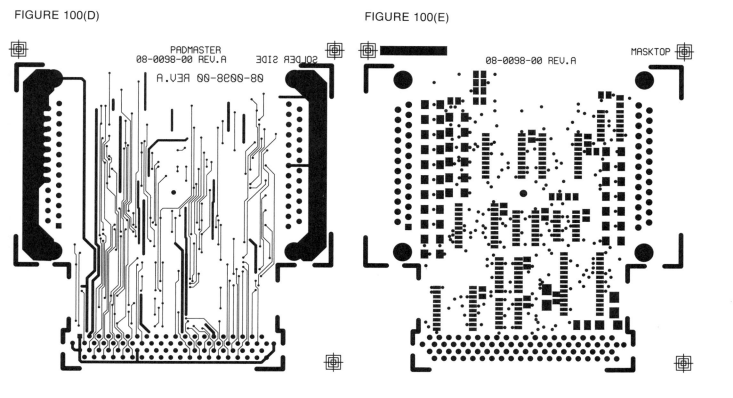

96

FIGURE 100(F)

FIGURE 100(G)

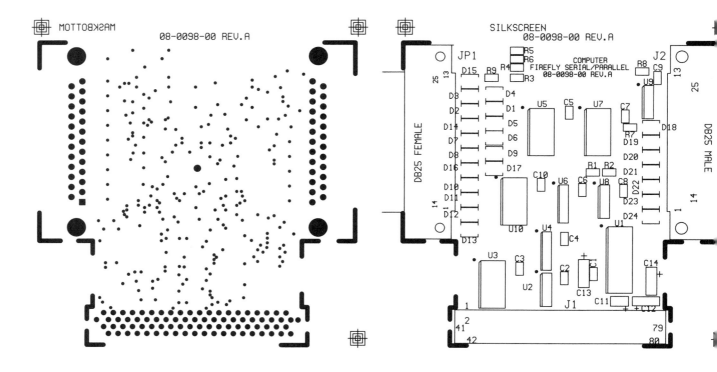

FIGURE 100(H)

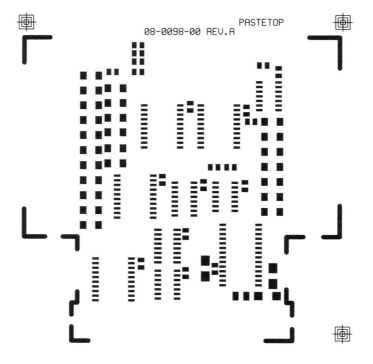

FIGURE 100(I)

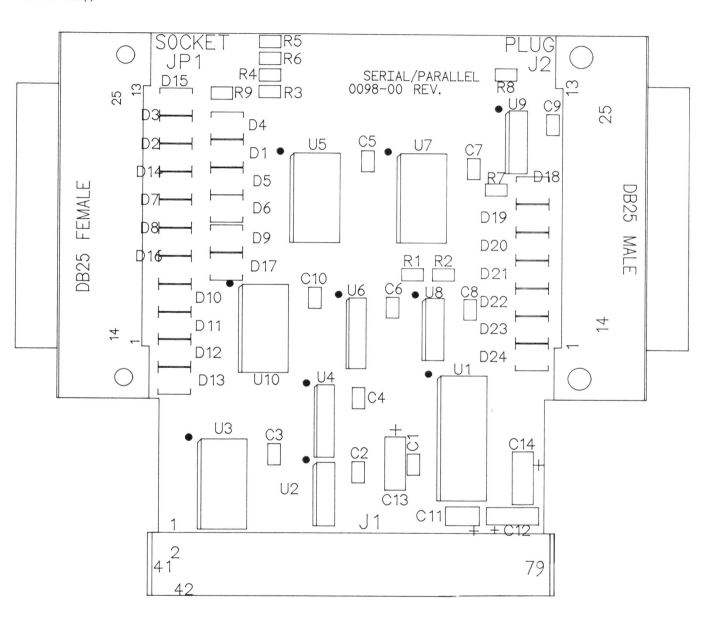

FIGURE 100(J)

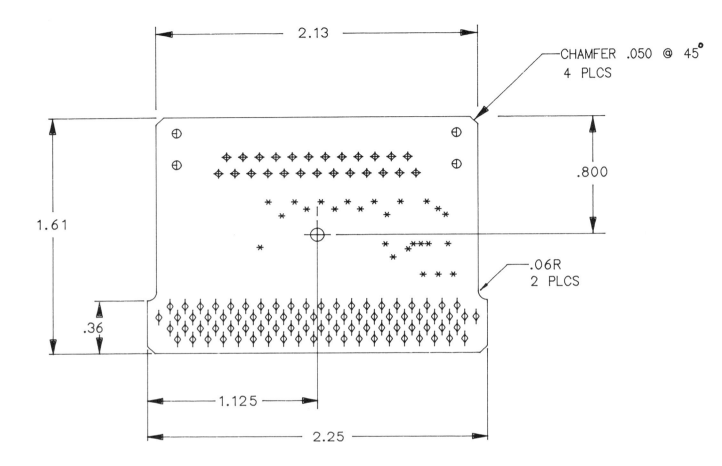

NOTES: UNLESS OTHERWISE SPECIFIED

1. MATERIAL: FR4 .062 FINISHED THICKNESS
   ONE OUNCE COPPER
   TWO LAYERS.

2. FINISH: SOLDER PLATE 60/40 TIN/LEAD OVER EXPOSED PADS
   AND COPPER .0003 –.0005.

3. SOLDER MASK BOTH SIDES.

4. ALL HOLES PLATED THRU.

5. SILKSCREEN, WHITE.

HOLE	CHART		
CODE	SIZE	QTY	PLATED
*	.020 +/−.003 DIA.	25	YES
◇	.032 +/−.003 DIA.	82	YES
⊕	.042 +/−.003 DIA.	25	YES
⊕	.166 +/−.005 DIA.	1	NO
⊕	.125 +/−.005 DIA.	4	NO

Worksheets

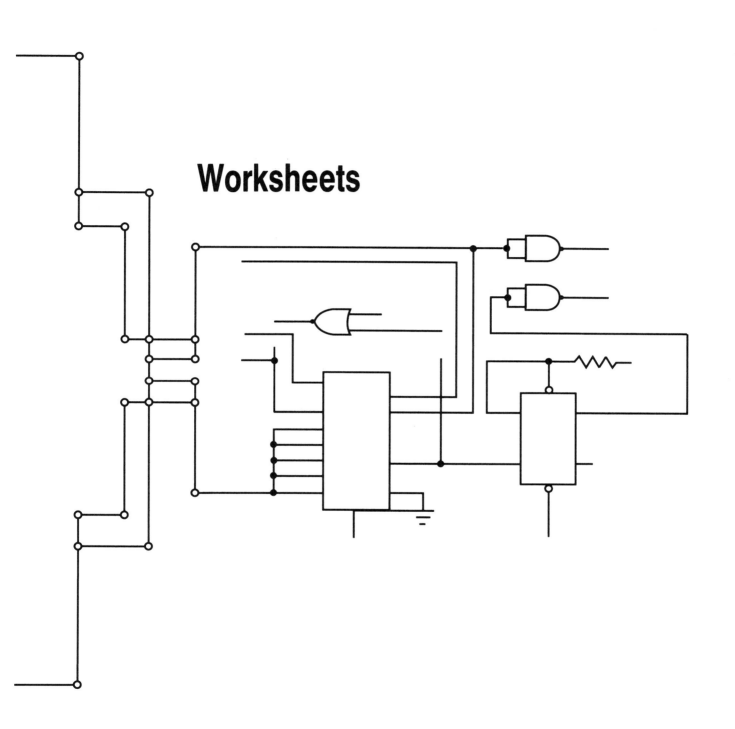

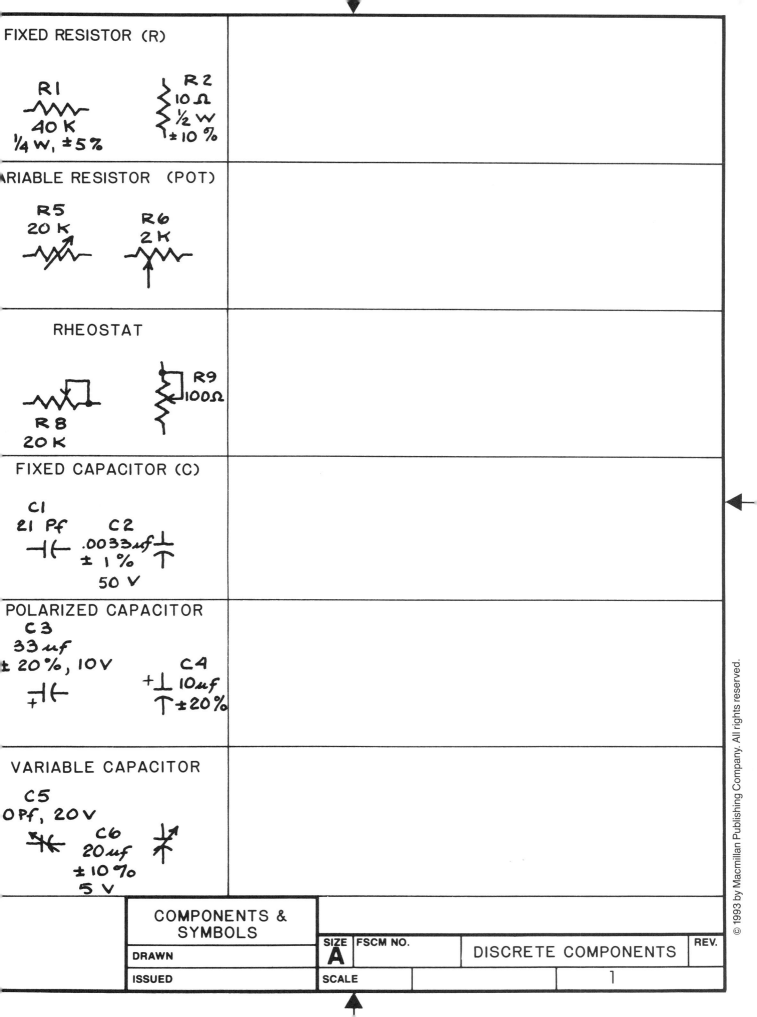

FIXED RESISTOR (R)

R1
40 K
¼ W, ±5%

R2
10 Ω
½ W
± 10 %

VARIABLE RESISTOR (POT)

R5
20 K

R6
2 K

RHEOSTAT

R8
20 K

R9
100 Ω

FIXED CAPACITOR (C)

C1
21 Pf

C2
.0033 μf
± 1 %
50 V

POLARIZED CAPACITOR

C3
33 μf
± 20 %, 10 V

C4
10 μf
±20%

VARIABLE CAPACITOR

C5
0 Pf, 20 V

C6
20 μf
± 10 %
5 V

COMPONENTS & SYMBOLS				
DRAWN	SIZE **A**	FSCM NO.	DISCRETE COMPONENTS	REV.
ISSUED	SCALE			1

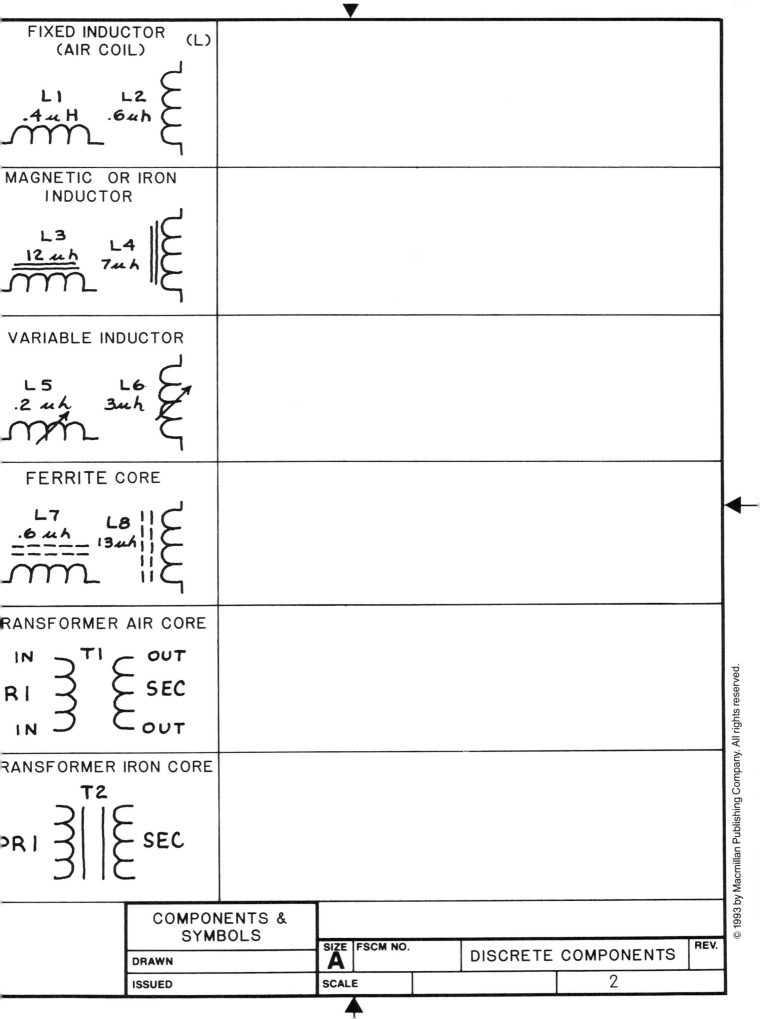

FIXED INDUCTOR (AIR COIL) (L)	
MAGNETIC OR IRON INDUCTOR	
VARIABLE INDUCTOR	
FERRITE CORE	
TRANSFORMER AIR CORE	
TRANSFORMER IRON CORE	

COMPONENTS & SYMBOLS

DRAWN

ISSUED

SIZE **A**

FSCM NO.

SCALE

DISCRETE COMPONENTS

REV.

2

POWER TRANSFORMER
MULTIPLE WINDING

T3

BLK

PRI

BLK

RED
CT
RED/YEL — HIGH VOLTAGE
RED

YEL
YEL — LOW VOLTAGE #1
GRN

CT
GRN/YEL — LOW VOLTAGE #2
GRN

EMI-CONDUCTOR DIODES
SIGNAL DIODE (CR)
(DI)

CR1
N4148

THODE
D

CR2
EJT
1100

ANODE
END

CR3
1N60

ZENER DIODE

CR4
1N 960
9V

CR5(ZR)
1N 5231
5 V
1W

TUNNEL DIODE

CR6

CR7

LED

(DS)
RED
3.5V

ODE BRIDGE OR RECTIFIER
1N4001

CR11

CR8
(-)

CR10

CR9

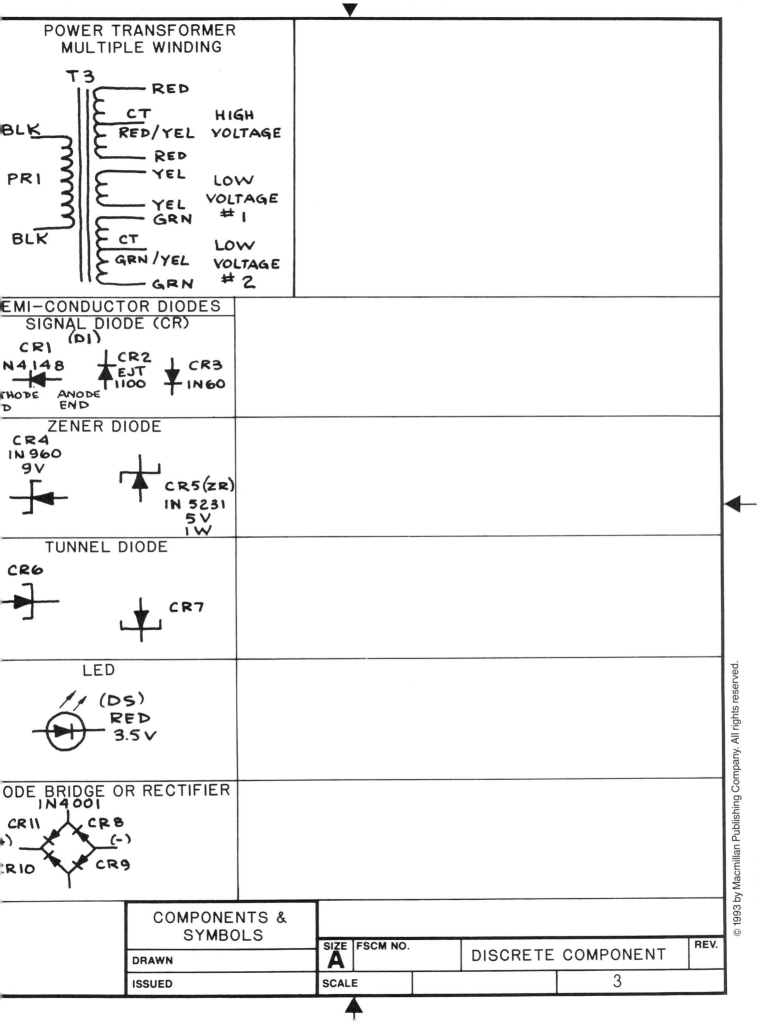

COMPONENTS & SYMBOLS				
DRAWN	SIZE **A**	FSCM NO.	DISCRETE COMPONENT	REV.
ISSUED	SCALE		3	

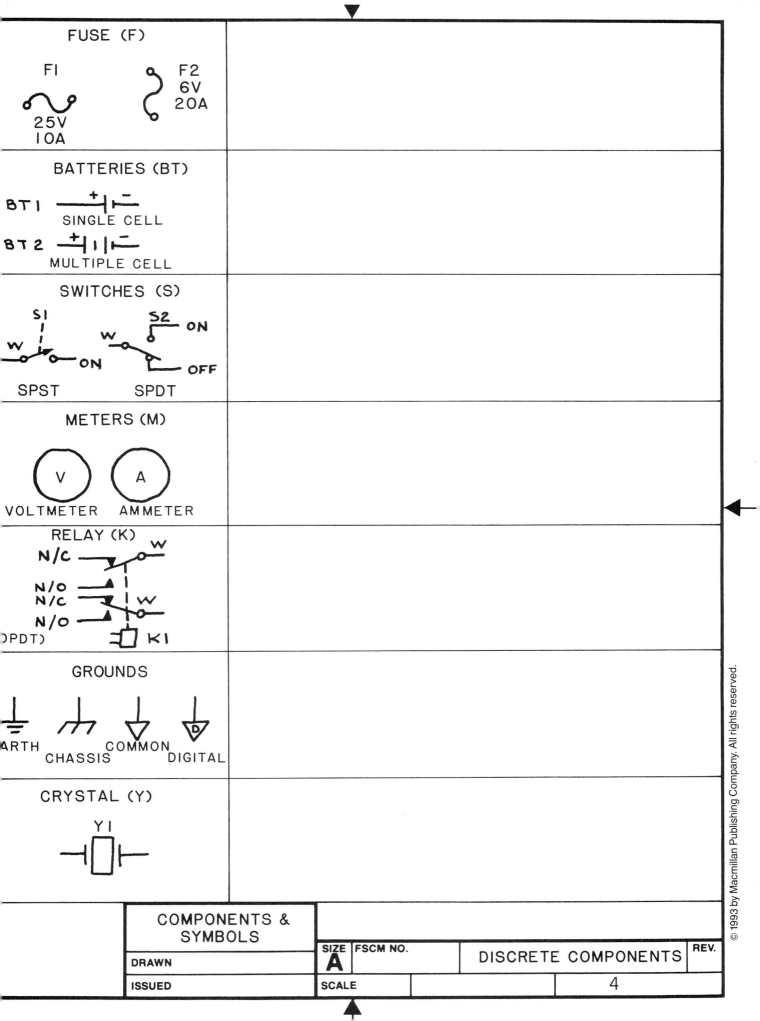

FUSE (F)

FI
25V
IOA

F2
6V
20A

BATTERIES (BT)

BT1 — SINGLE CELL

BT2 — MULTIPLE CELL

SWITCHES (S)

SI
W — ON
SPST

S2
W — ON
OFF
SPDT

METERS (M)

V
VOLTMETER

A
AMMETER

RELAY (K)

N/C — W
N/O
N/C — W
N/O
(DPDT) — KI

GROUNDS

ARTH

CHASSIS

COMMON

D
DIGITAL

CRYSTAL (Y)

YI

COMPONENTS & SYMBOLS				
DRAWN	SIZE A	FSCM NO.	DISCRETE COMPONENTS	REV.
ISSUED	SCALE		4	

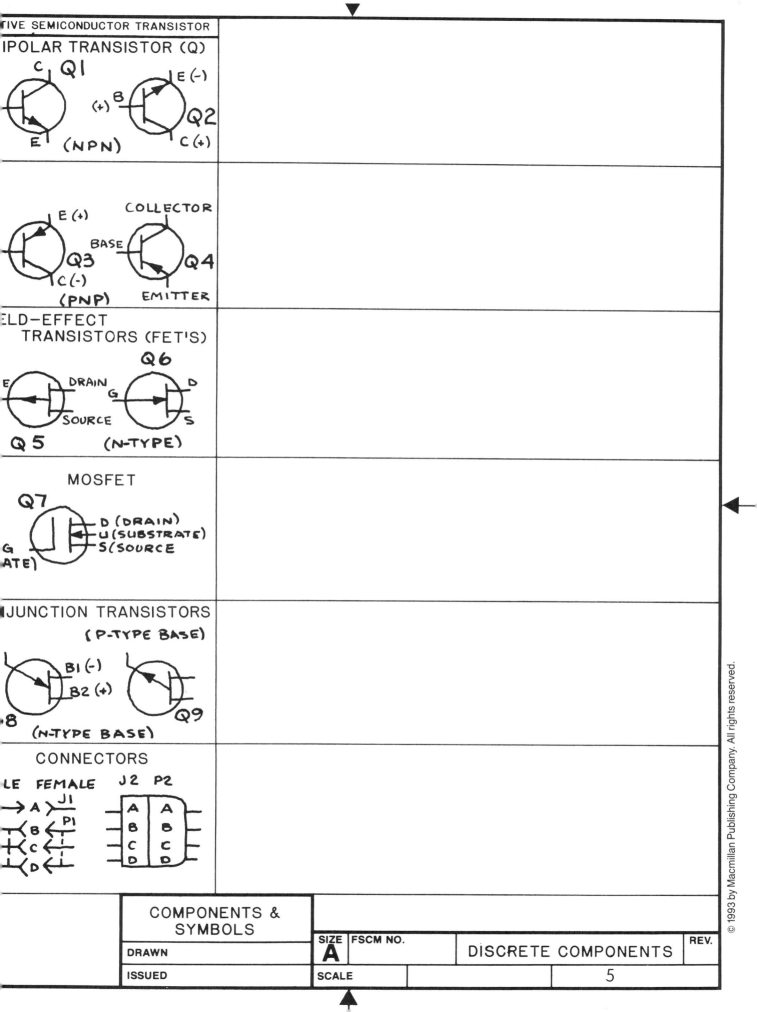

ACTIVE SEMICONDUCTOR TRANSISTOR

BIPOLAR TRANSISTOR (Q)

C Q1
E
(NPN)

E (-)
(+) B
Q2
C (+)

E (+)
BASE
Q3
C (-)
(PNP)

COLLECTOR
Q4
EMITTER

FIELD-EFFECT
TRANSISTORS (FET'S)

Q6

E DRAIN
SOURCE
Q5

G D
S
(N-TYPE)

MOSFET

Q7
D (DRAIN)
U (SUBSTRATE)
S (SOURCE)
G
(GATE)

UNIJUNCTION TRANSISTORS
(P-TYPE BASE)

B1 (-)
B2 (+)
Q8
(N-TYPE BASE)

Q9

CONNECTORS

MALE FEMALE   J2 P2

A J1
B P1
C
D

A   A
B   B
C   C
D   D

COMPONENTS & SYMBOLS			
DRAWN	SIZE **A**	FSCM NO.	DISCRETE COMPONENTS	REV.
ISSUED	SCALE		5

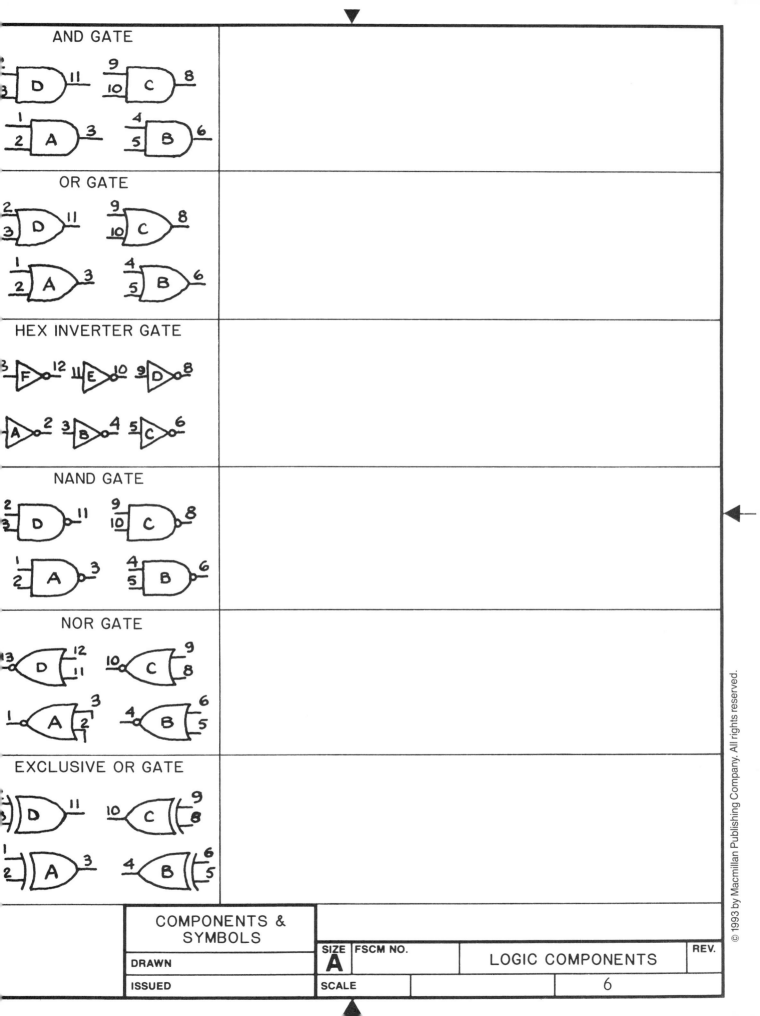

AND GATE

OR GATE

HEX INVERTER GATE

NAND GATE

NOR GATE

EXCLUSIVE OR GATE

COMPONENTS & SYMBOLS			
DRAWN	SIZE A	FSCM NO.	LOGIC COMPONENTS	REV.
ISSUED	SCALE		6	

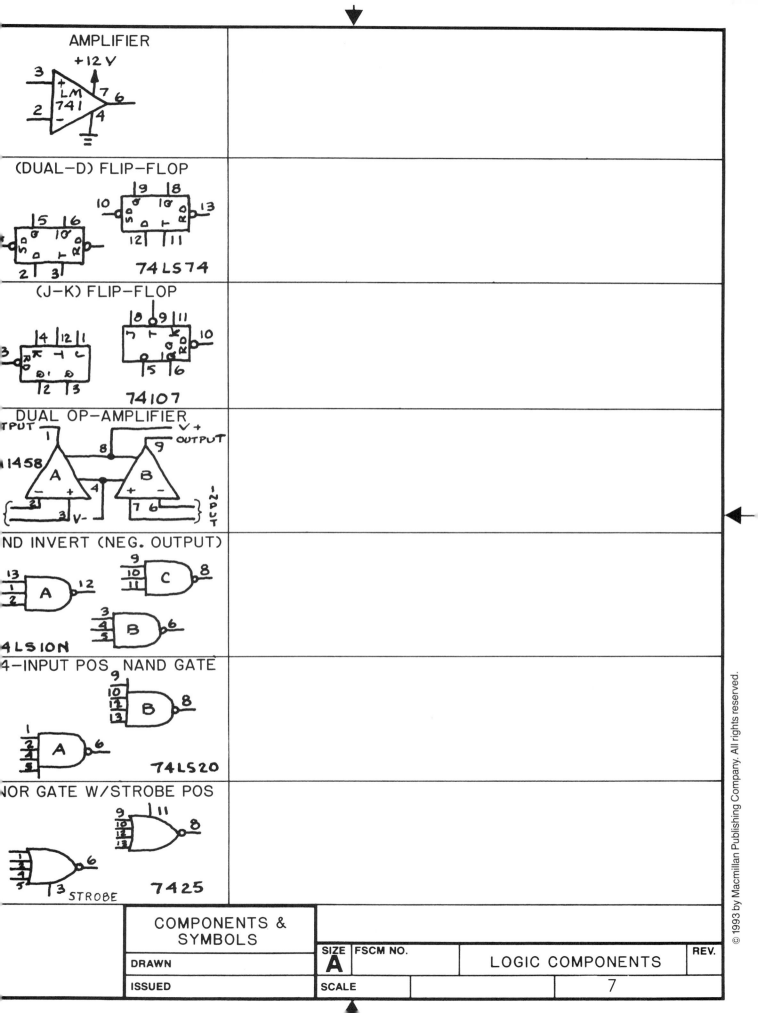

AMPLIFIER

+12 V

LM 741

(DUAL-D) FLIP-FLOP

74LS74

(J-K) FLIP-FLOP

74107

DUAL OP-AMPLIFIER

INPUT

V +
OUTPUT

1458

A   B

V-
INPUT

AND INVERT (NEG. OUTPUT)

A   C   B

74LS10N

4-INPUT POS NAND GATE

B

A

74LS20

NOR GATE W/STROBE POS

STROBE   7425

COMPONENTS & SYMBOLS

DRAWN

ISSUED

SIZE **A**   FSCM NO.

SCALE

LOGIC COMPONENTS

REV.

7

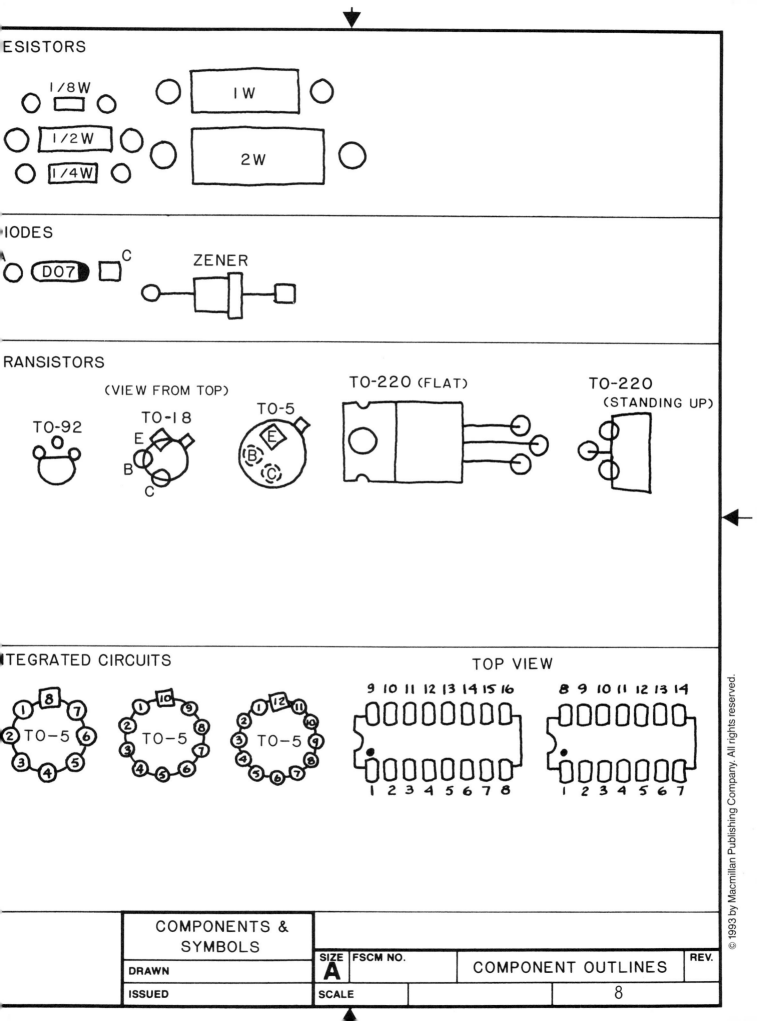

RESISTORS

1/8W
1W
1/2W
2W
1/4W

DIODES

DO7 C

ZENER

TRANSISTORS

(VIEW FROM TOP)

TO-92

TO-18
E
B
C

TO-5
E
B
C

TO-220 (FLAT)

TO-220 (STANDING UP)

INTEGRATED CIRCUITS

TOP VIEW

8
1   7
2 TO-5 6
3   5
4

10
1   9
2   8
3 TO-5 7
4   6
5

12
1   11
2   10
3 TO-5 9
4   8
5
6

9 10 11 12 13 14 15 16

1 2 3 4 5 6 7 8

8 9 10 11 12 13 14

1 2 3 4 5 6 7

COMPONENTS & SYMBOLS				
DRAWN	SIZE **A**	FSCM NO.	COMPONENT OUTLINES	REV.
ISSUED	SCALE		8	

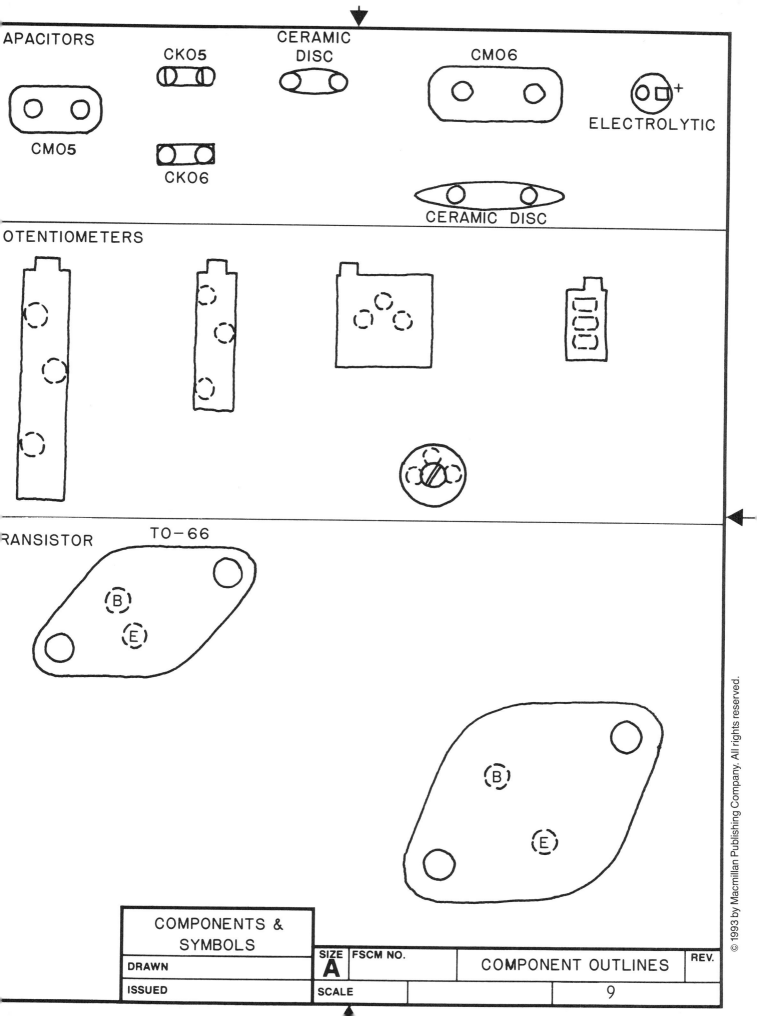

APACITORS

CKO5

CERAMIC
DISC

CMO6

CMO5

CKO6

ELECTROLYTIC

CERAMIC DISC

OTENTIOMETERS

RANSISTOR   TO-66

B

E

B

E

COMPONENTS & SYMBOLS				
DRAWN	SIZE **A**	FSCM NO.	COMPONENT OUTLINES	REV.
ISSUED	SCALE		9	

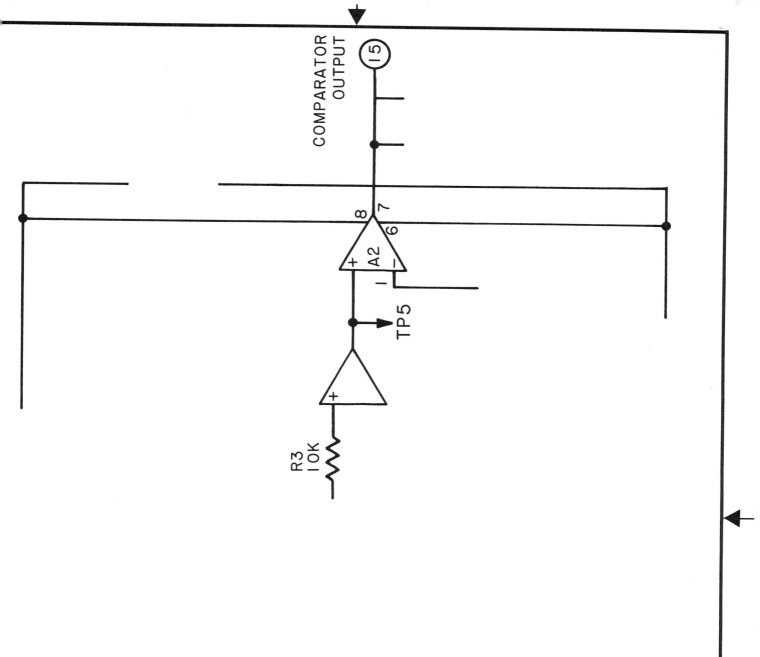

COMPARATOR OUTPUT

15

8 7

+ A2 −

TP5

R3
10K

SCHEMATIC DIAGRAMS

| DRAWN | SIZE **A** | FSCM NO. | ANALOG COMPARATOR | REV. |
| ISSUED | SCALE | | 10 | |

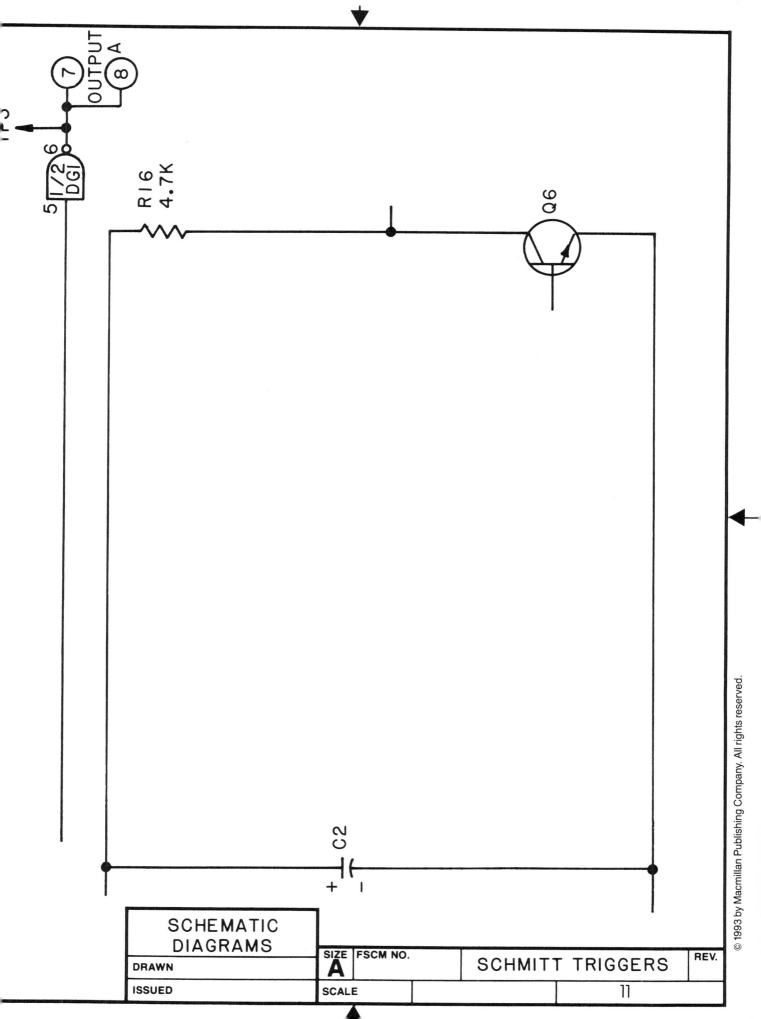

OUTPUT A

7 ⑧

TP3

5 6
1/2
DGI

R16
4.7K

Q6

C2
+ —

SCHEMATIC
DIAGRAMS

DRAWN

ISSUED

SIZE **A** | FSCM NO.

SCALE

SCHMITT TRIGGERS

REV.

11

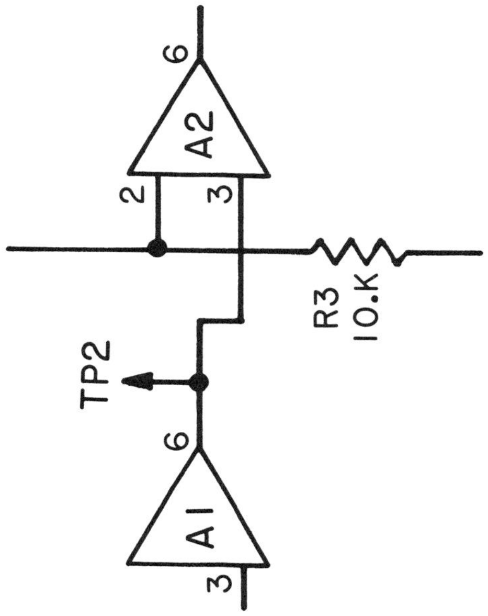

SCHEMATIC DIAGRAMS

| DRAWN | SIZE
A | FSCM NO. | BUFFER AMPLIFIER | REV. |
| ISSUED | SCALE | | 12 | |

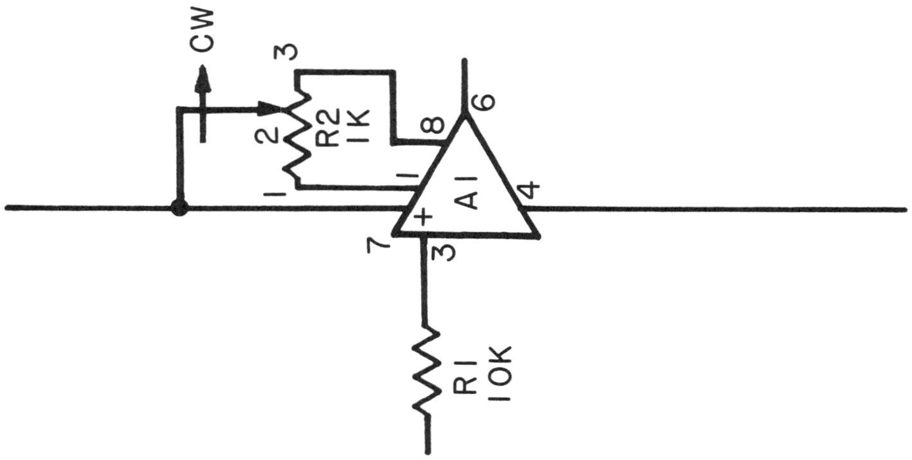

CW

R2
1K

3
2

8

6

A1

1

4

+

7
3

R1
10K

SCHEMATIC DIAGRAMS

DRAWN

ISSUED

SIZE
A

FSCM NO.

SCALE

OPERATIONAL AMPLIFIER

REV.

13

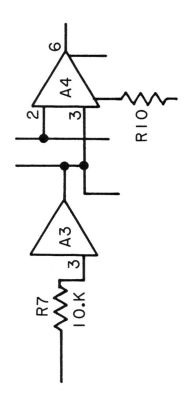

SCHEMATIC DIAGRAMS				
DRAWN	SIZE **A**	FSCM NO.	AMPLIFIER	REV.
ISSUED	SCALE		14	

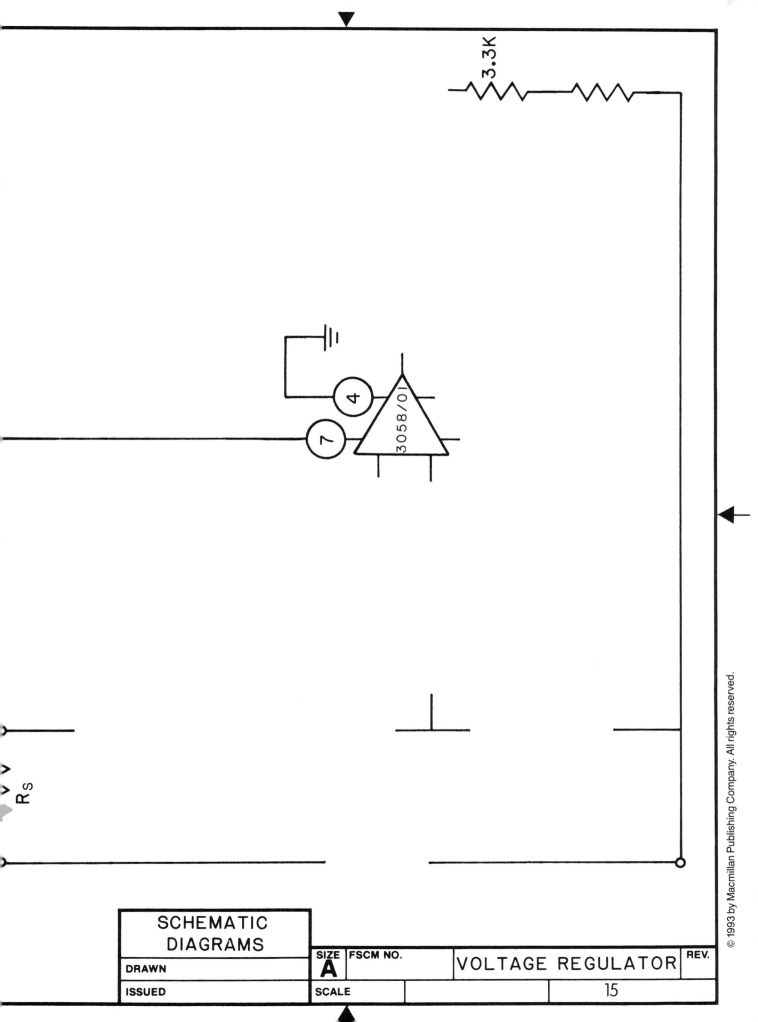

3.3K

3058/01

4

7

R$_S$

SCHEMATIC
DIAGRAMS

DRAWN	SIZE **A**	FSCM NO.	VOLTAGE REGULATOR	REV.
ISSUED	SCALE		15	

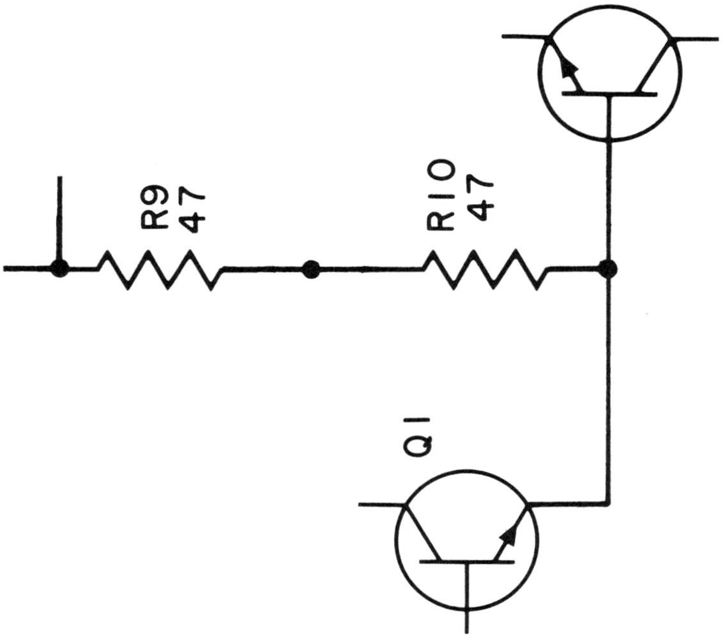

SCHEMATIC DIAGRAMS

DRAWN	SIZE **A**	FSCM NO.
ISSUED	SCALE	

2KV NEGATIVE POWER SUPPLY

REV.

16

R9
47

R10
47

Q1

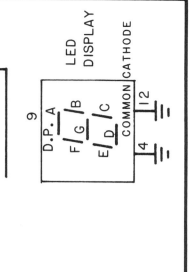

LED DISPLAY

COMMON CATHODE

D.P. A
F G B
E D C

9

12

4

AND

V_CC

8

9 10

3 5

11

6 4

SCHEMATIC DIAGRAMS				
	SIZE	FSCM NO.		REV.
DRAWN	**A**		DIGITAL METER	
ISSUED	SCALE		17	

	SIZE	FSCM NO.		REV.
DRAWN	**A**			
ISSUED	SCALE		18	

IN ———

IN ———

	SIZE	FSCM NO.		REV.
DRAWN	**A**			
ISSUED	SCALE		19	

A O——

B O——

	SIZE	FSCM NO.		REV.
DRAWN	**A**			
ISSUED	SCALE		20	

	SIZE	FSCM NO.		REV.
DRAWN	**A**			
ISSUED	SCALE		21	

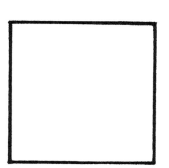

	SIZE	FSCM NO.		REV.
DRAWN	**A**			
ISSUED	SCALE		22	

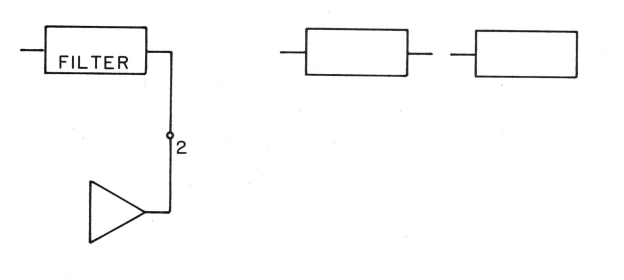

FILTER

2

TWIN-T
FILTER L

R

BLOCK DIAGRAMS

		SIZE	FSCM NO.		REV.
DRAWN		**A**		TRANSISTOR FUNCTIONS	
ISSUED		SCALE			23

TEST
STA
A

⌐———————— HEADQUARTERS PLANT ————————┐

BLOCK DIAGRAMS					
DRAWN	SIZE **A**	FSCM NO.	TELECOMMUNICATIONS		REV.
ISSUED	SCALE			24	

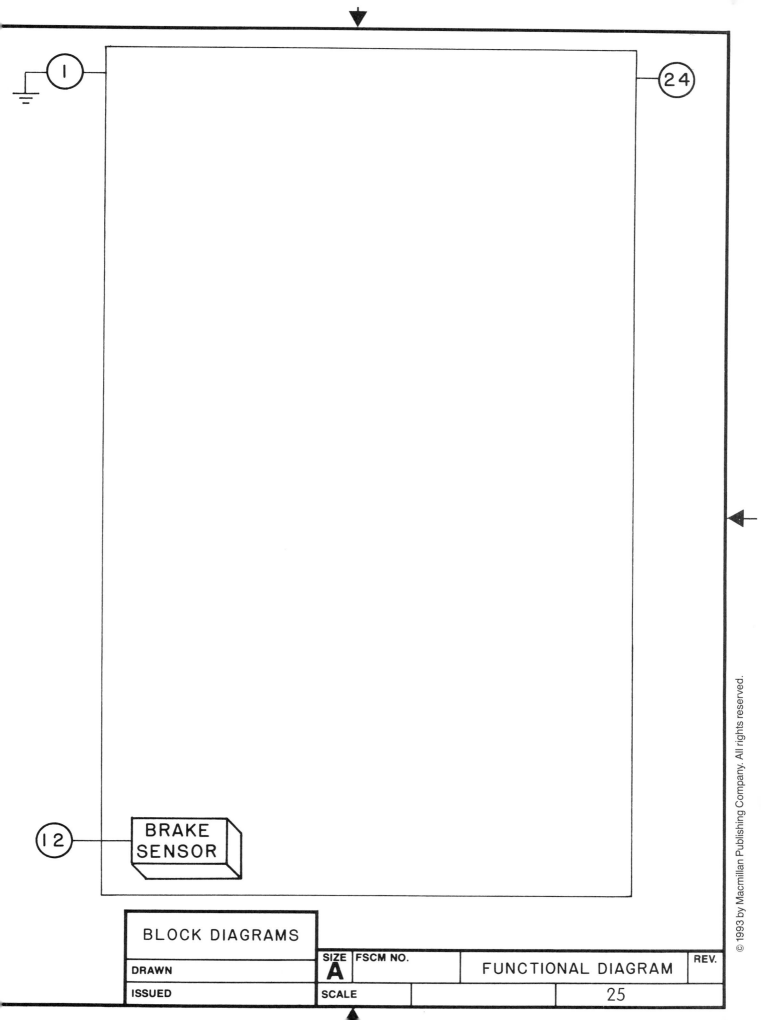

①

⑫ BRAKE
SENSOR

㉔

BLOCK DIAGRAMS

DRAWN	SIZE **A**	FSCM NO.	FUNCTIONAL DIAGRAM	REV.
ISSUED	SCALE		25	

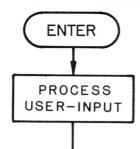

ENTER

PROCESS
USER–INPUT

FROM
ALLOCATION
STACK

BLOCK DIAGRAMS				
DRAWN	SIZE **A**	FSCM NO.	DATA ANALYZER	REV.
ISSUED	SCALE		26	

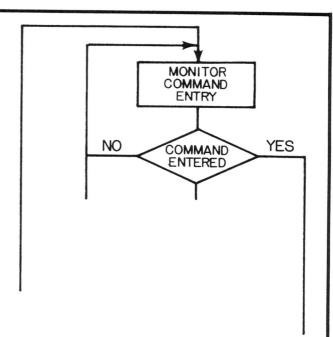

```
        ┌──────────────────┐
        │     MONITOR      │
        │     COMMAND      │
        │      ENTRY       │
        └──────────────────┘

NO        ◇ COMMAND ◇        YES
          ◇ ENTERED ◇
```

BLOCK DIAGRAMS					
DRAWN	SIZE **A**	FSCM NO.	MONITOR PROGRAM		REV.
ISSUED	SCALE			27	

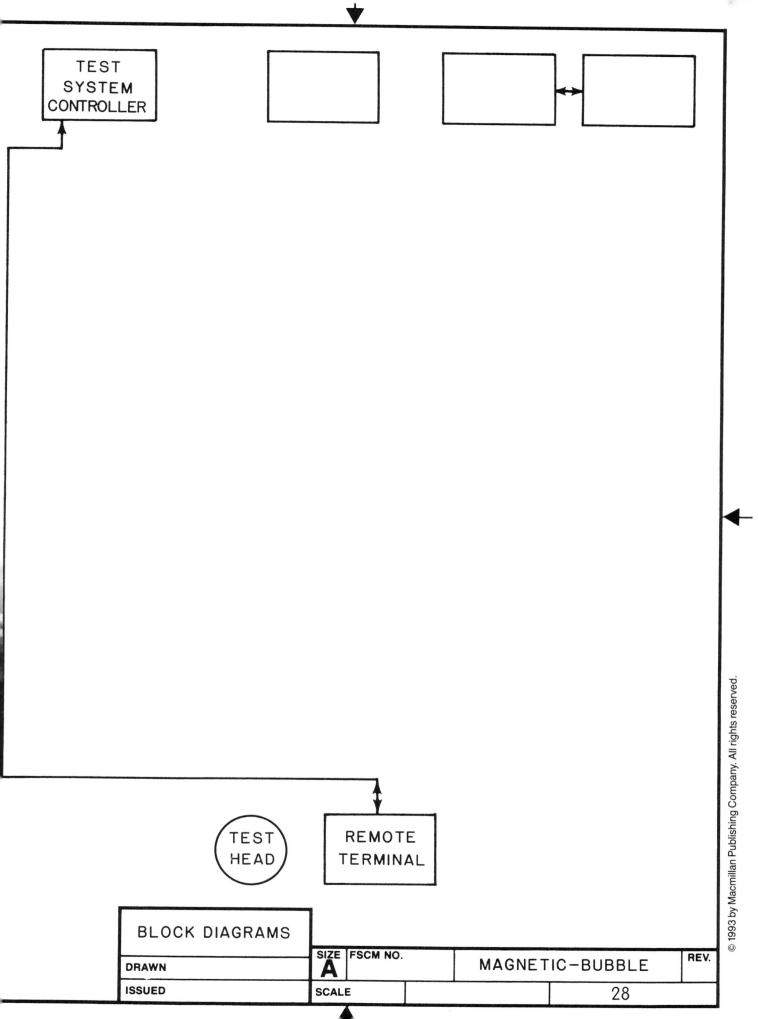

TEST
SYSTEM
CONTROLLER

TEST
HEAD

REMOTE
TERMINAL

BLOCK DIAGRAMS

DRAWN

ISSUED

SIZE **A**	FSCM NO.	MAGNETIC–BUBBLE	REV.
SCALE		28	

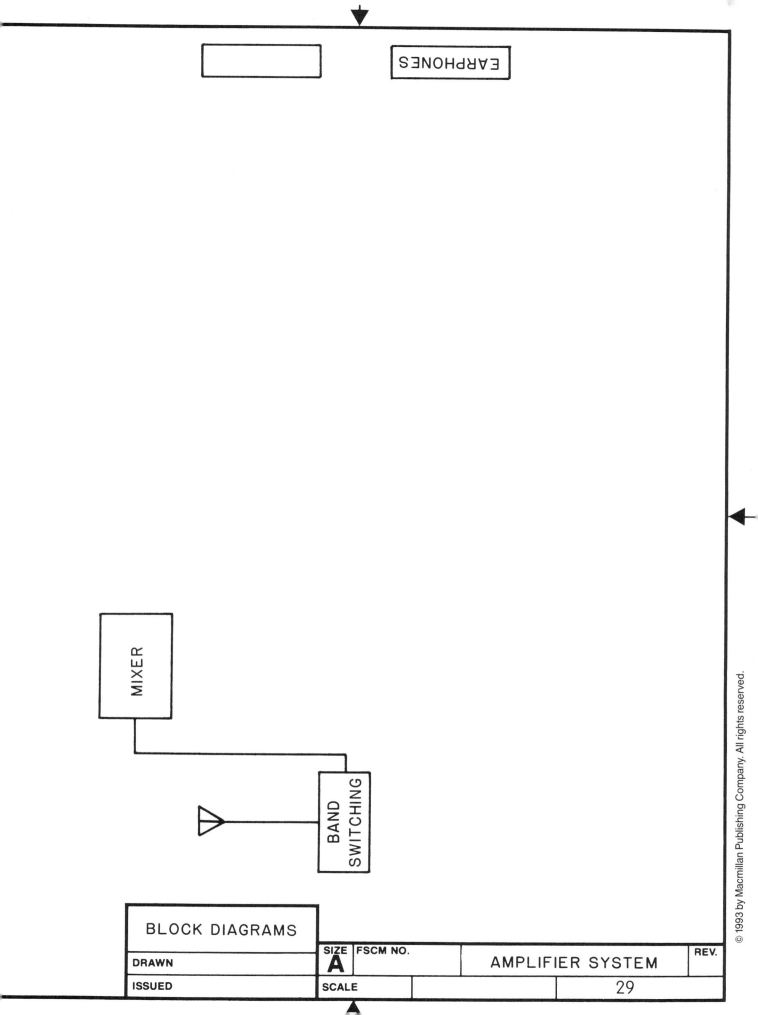

EARPHONES

MIXER

BAND SWITCHING

BLOCK DIAGRAMS

DRAWN	SIZE **A**	FSCM NO.		AMPLIFIER SYSTEM	REV.
ISSUED	SCALE			29	

```
┌─────────────────────────────────────────────────────────────────────────────┐
│                                                                         REV.  │
│                                                                               │
│                                                                               │
│                                           30                                  │
│                                                                               │
│                                                                               │
│                                                                               │
│                                                                               │
│                                                                               │
│                    ┌─────────────────────────────────┐                        │
│                    │                                 │                        │
│                    │           CONTROLLER            │                        │
│                    │                                 │                        │
│                    └─────────────────────────────────┘                        │
│       ┌──────────────────────────────┐                                        │
│       │                              │                                        │
│       ├──────────────────────────────┤────┬──────────┬──────────────┬────────│
│       │ DRAWN                        │SIZE│FSCM NO.  │              │  REV.  │
│       │                              │ A  │          │              │        │
│       ├──────────────────────────────┼────┴──────────┼───────┬──────────────│
│       │ ISSUED                       │ SCALE         │       │      30       │
└───────┴──────────────────────────────┴───────────────┴───────┴──────────────┘
```

FROM CONTROLLER

	SIZE **A**	**FSCM NO.**		**REV.**
DRAWN				
ISSUED	**SCALE**		31	

FROM CONTROLLER

	SIZE	FSCM NO.		REV.
DRAWN	A			
ISSUED	SCALE		32	

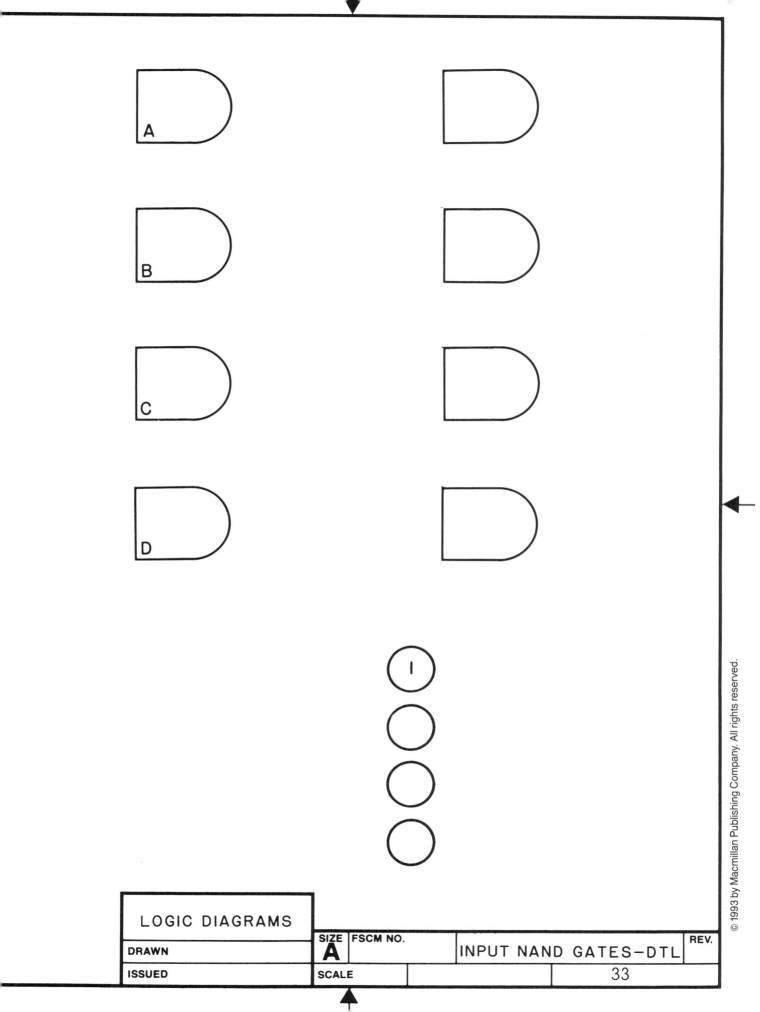

LOGIC DIAGRAMS

DRAWN

ISSUED

SIZE
A

FSCM NO.

SCALE

INPUT NAND GATES-DTL

REV.

33

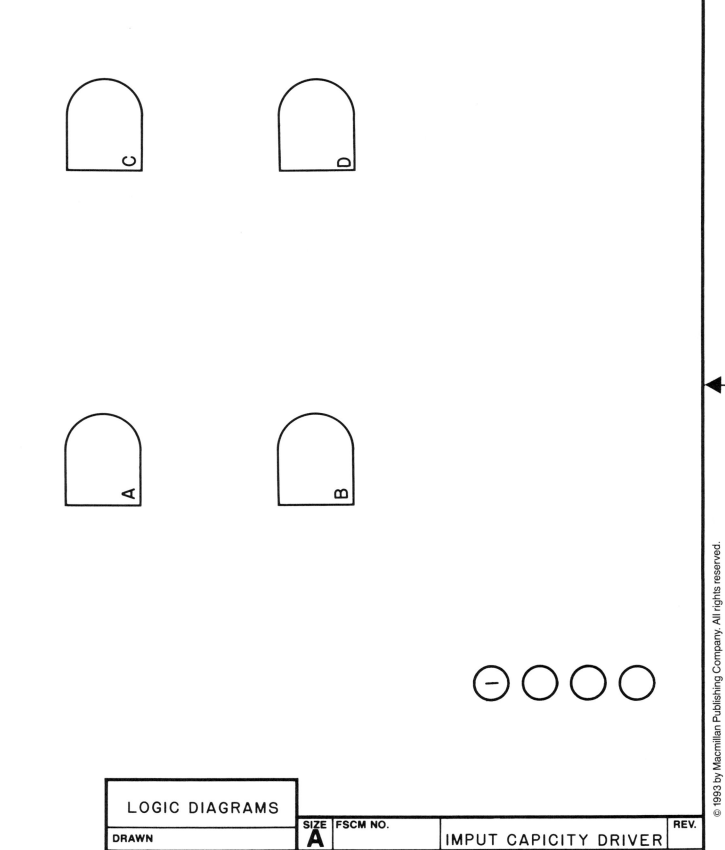

LOGIC DIAGRAMS

DRAWN

ISSUED

SIZE
A

FSCM NO.

SCALE

IMPUT CAPICITY DRIVER

REV.

34

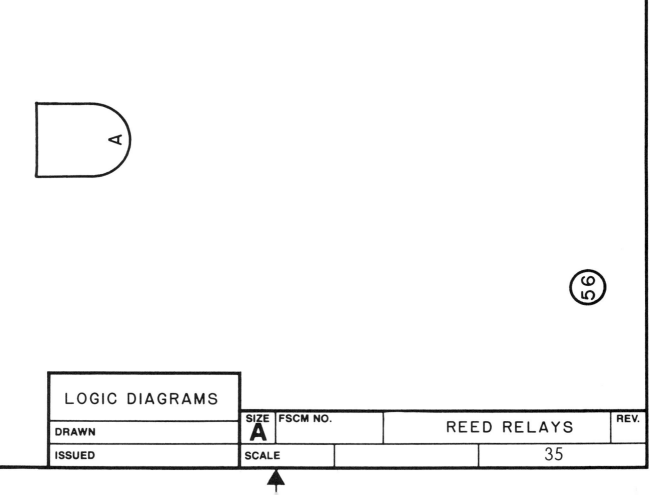

56

LOGIC DIAGRAMS

DRAWN	SIZE **A**	FSCM NO.	REED RELAYS	REV.
ISSUED	SCALE		35	

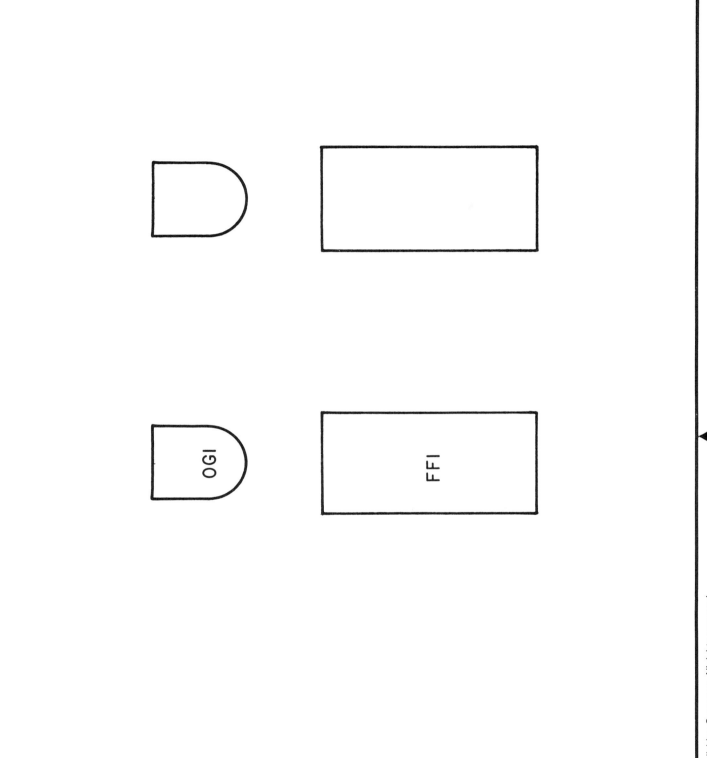

LOGIC DIAGRAMS

DRAWN

ISSUED

SIZE
A

FSCM NO.

SCALE

SHIFT   REGISTER

REV.

36

AI-A

LED 1

LOGIC DIAGRAMS				
DRAWN	SIZE **A**	FSCM NO.	FLASHER CIRCUITS	REV.
ISSUED	SCALE		37	

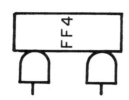

LOGIC DIAGRAMS				
DRAWN	**SIZE** **A**	**FSCM NO.**	CLOCK STORAGE	**REV.**
ISSUED	**SCALE**		38	

Q10

GRD

LOGIC DIAGRAMS				
DRAWN	SIZE **A**	FSCM NO.	LINE DRIVER	REV.
ISSUED	SCALE		39	

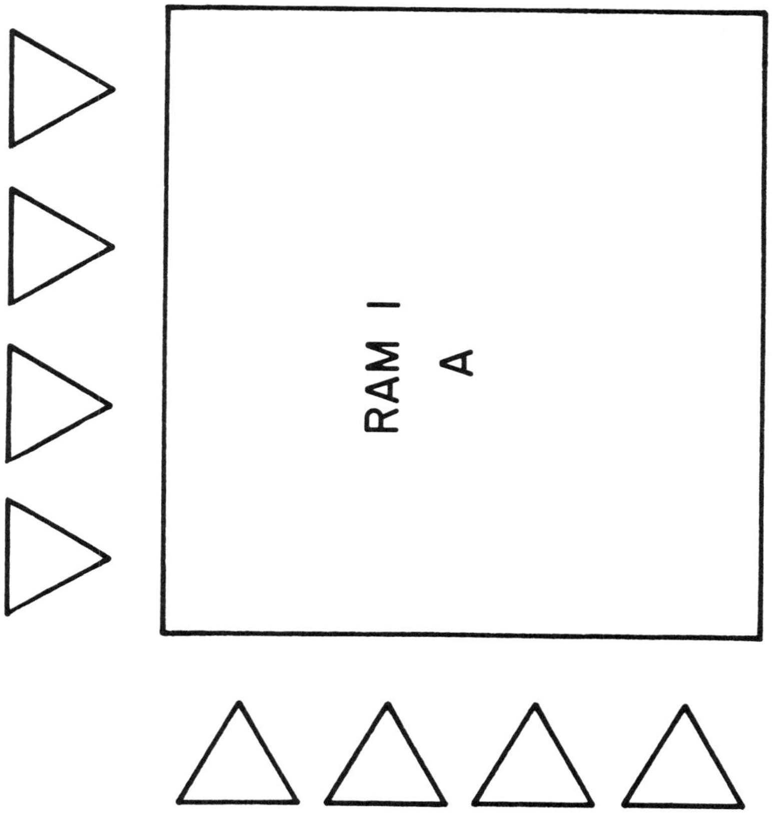

RAM I
A

LOGIC DIAGRAMS

DRAWN

ISSUED

SIZE **A**

FSCM NO.

SCALE

RANDOM ACCESS MEMORY

REV.

40

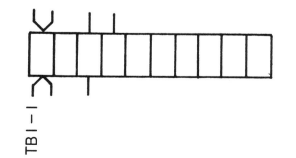

TBI-I

WIRING DIAGRAMS

| DRAWN | | | |
| ISSUED | | | |

| SIZE **A** | FSCM NO. | CONTROL PANEL | REV. |
| SCALE | | SHEET 41 | |

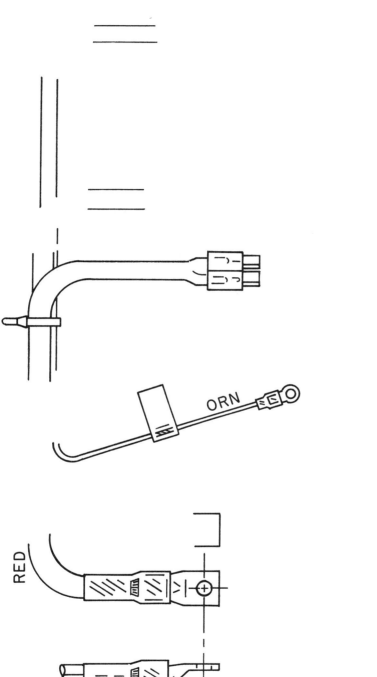

ORN

RED

RED
4 2
3 1
BLK

WIRING DIAGRAMS				
DRAWN	SIZE **A**	FSCM NO.	WIRE HARNESS ASS'Y	REV.
ISSUED	SCALE		42	

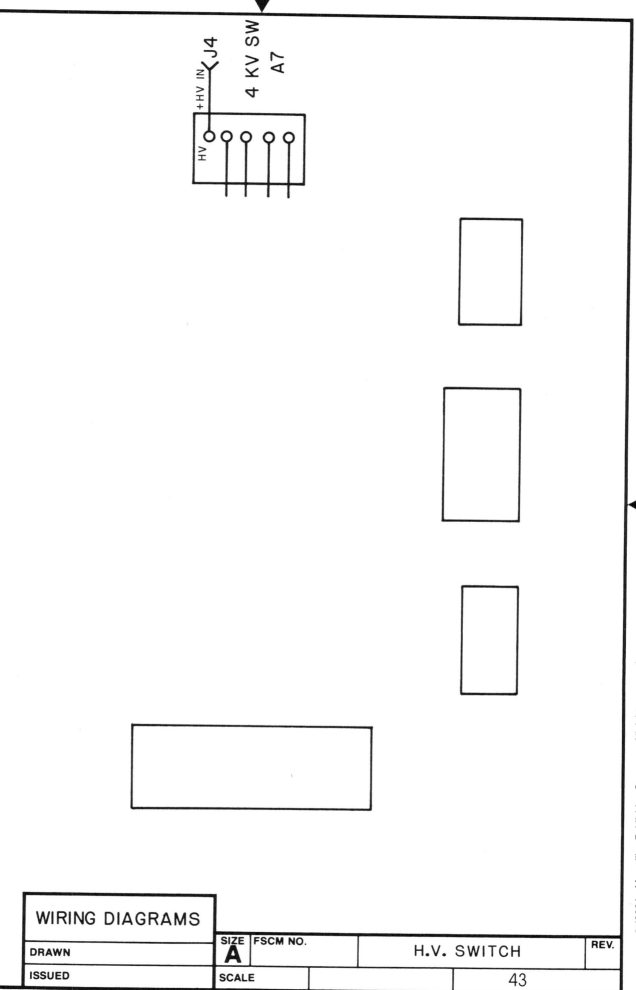

WIRING DIAGRAMS

DRAWN	**SIZE** **A**	**FSCM NO.**	H.V. SWITCH	**REV.**
ISSUED	**SCALE**		43	

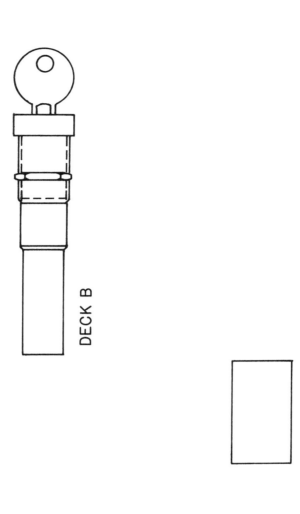

DECK B

NOTES: UNLESS OTHERWISE SPECIFIED

WIRING DIAGRAMS				
DRAWN	SIZE **A**	FSCM NO.	KEY SWITCH	REV.
ISSUED	SCALE		44	

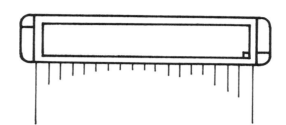

NOTES

WIRING DIAGRAMS				
DRAWN	SIZE **A**	FSCM NO.	FLAT CABLE	REV.
ISSUED	SCALE		45	

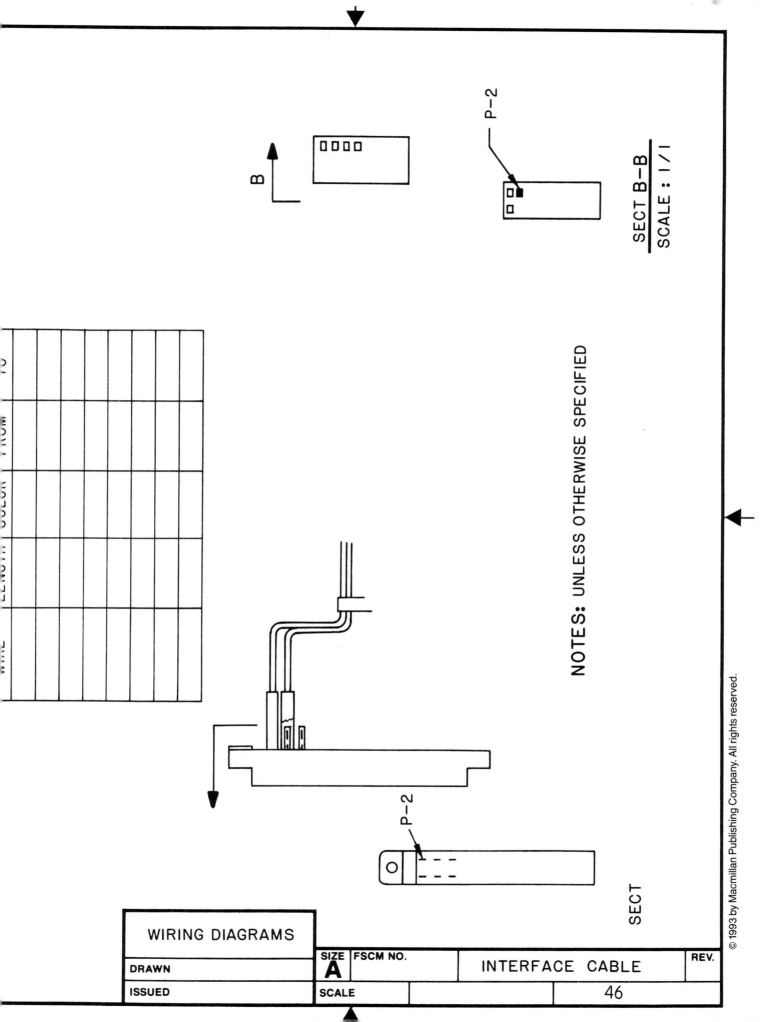

B

P-2

SECT B–B
SCALE : 1/1

NOTES: UNLESS OTHERWISE SPECIFIED

P-2

SECT

WIRING DIAGRAMS				
DRAWN	SIZE **A**	FSCM NO.	INTERFACE CABLE	REV.
ISSUED	SCALE		46	

RADIO

DRAWN	SIZE A	FSCM NO.		REV.
ISSUED	SCALE		47	

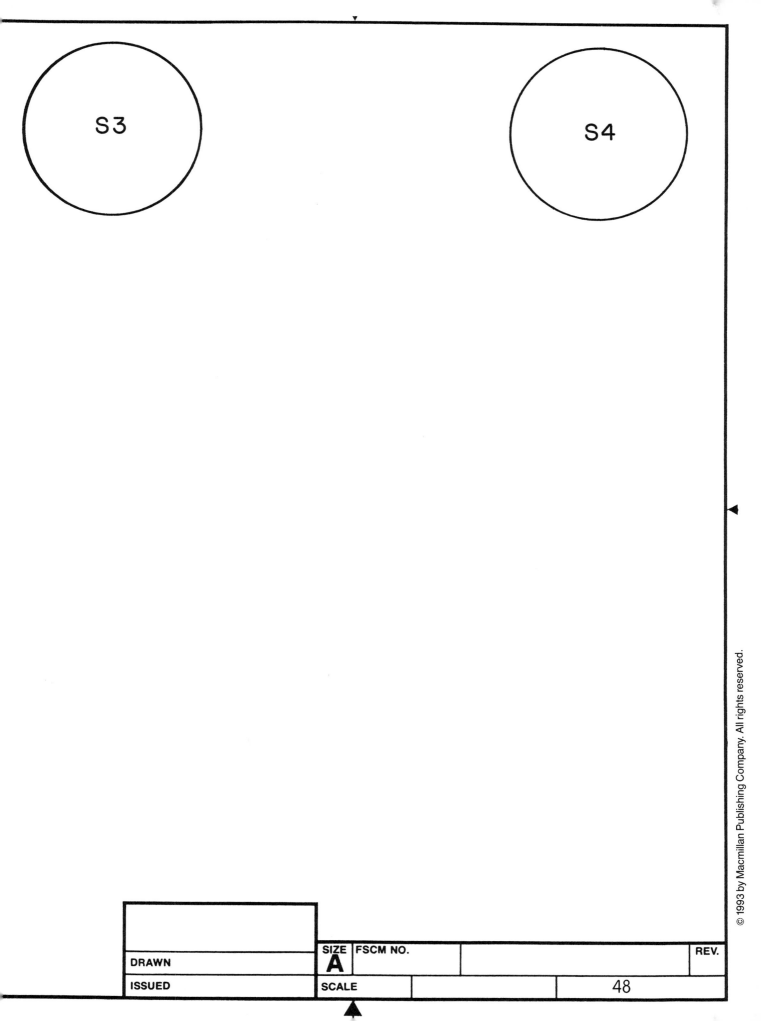

S3

S4

	SIZE **A**	FSCM NO.		REV.
DRAWN				
ISSUED	SCALE		48	

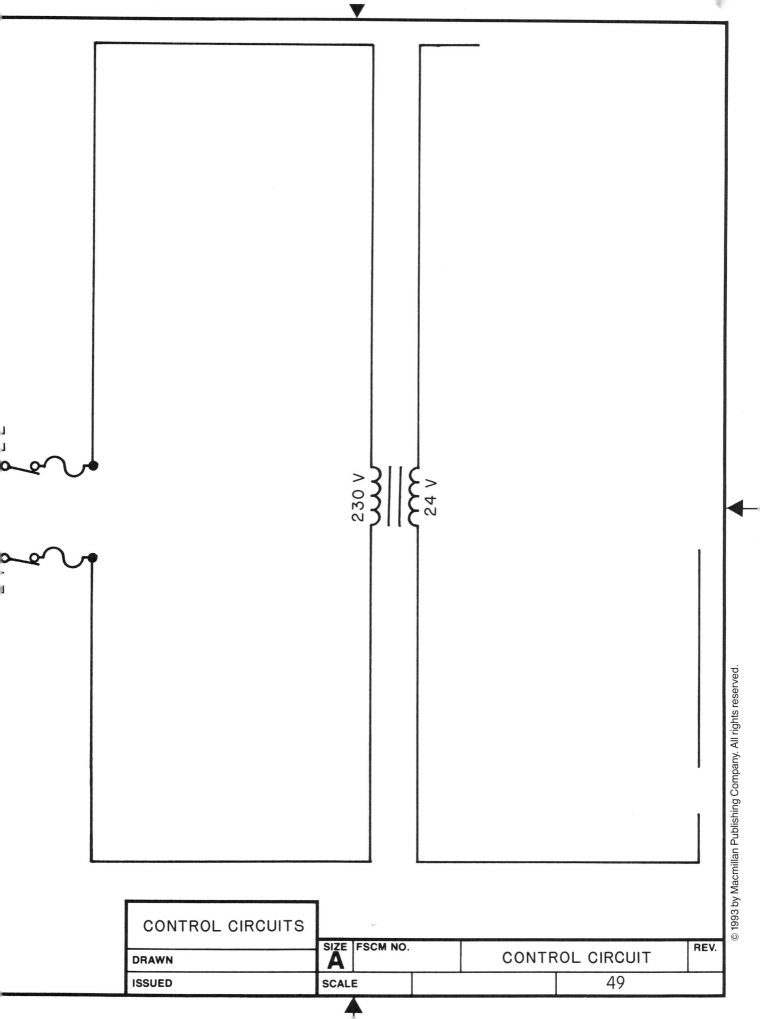

230 V 24 V

CONTROL CIRCUITS

DRAWN	SIZE **A**	FSCM NO.	CONTROL CIRCUIT	REV.
ISSUED	SCALE		49	

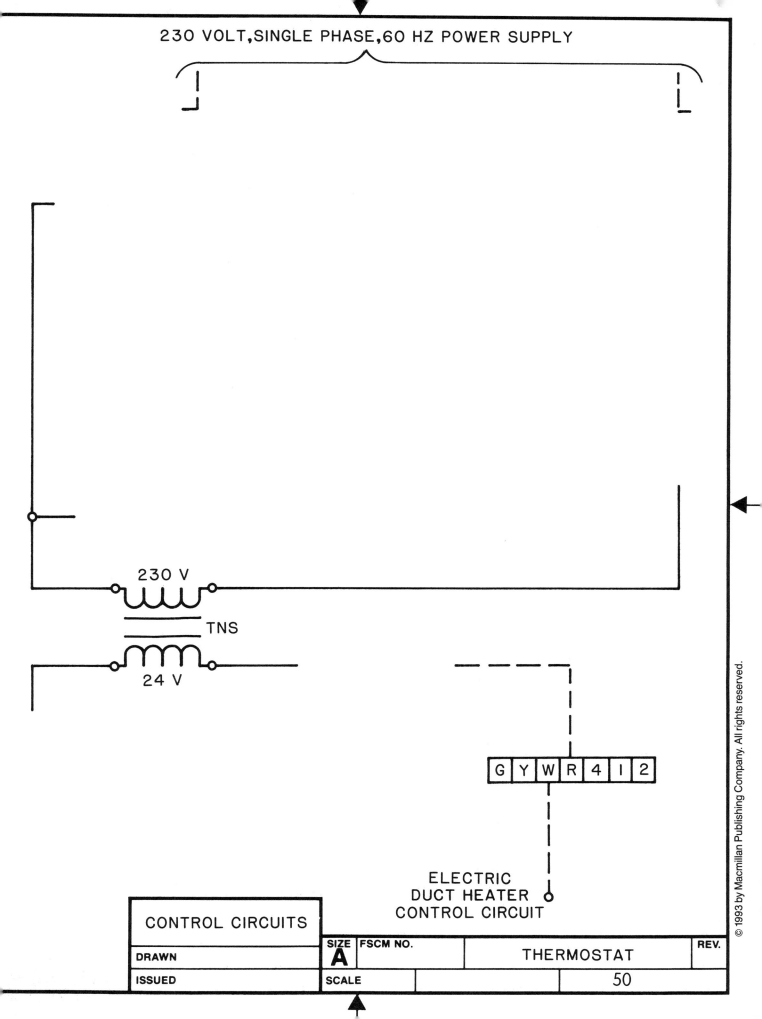

230 VOLT, SINGLE PHASE, 60 HZ POWER SUPPLY

230 V

TNS

24 V

G Y W R 4 1 2

ELECTRIC
DUCT HEATER
CONTROL CIRCUIT

CONTROL CIRCUITS				
DRAWN	SIZE **A**	FSCM NO.	THERMOSTAT	REV.
ISSUED	SCALE		50	

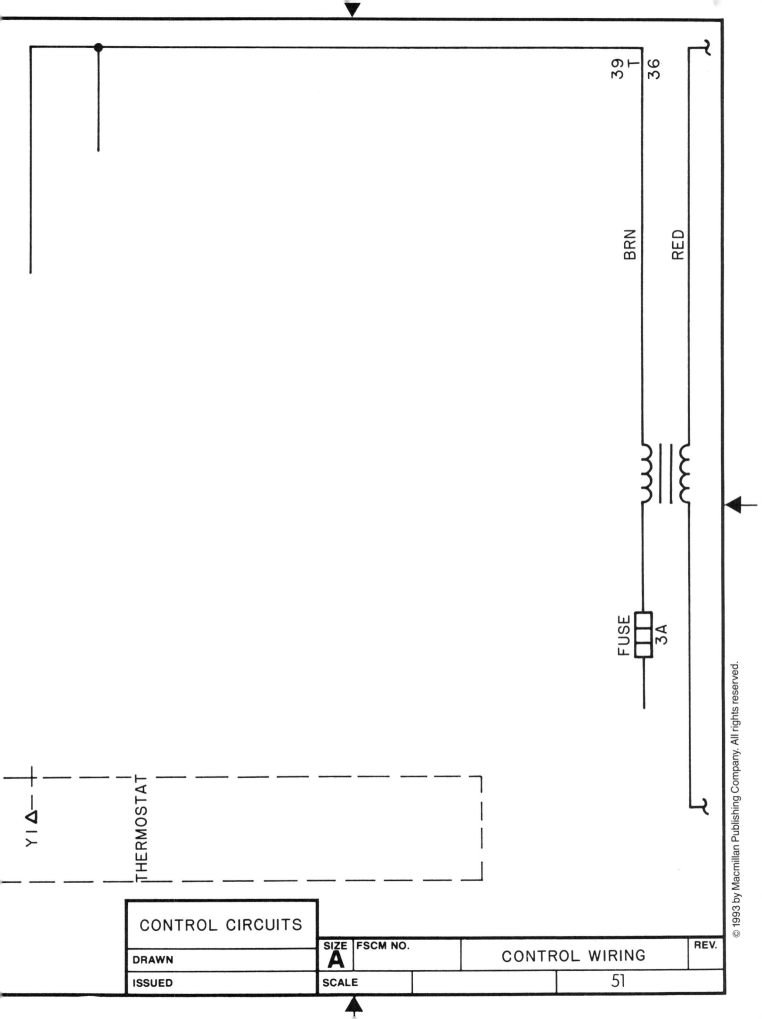

Y1 ⊿

THERMOSTAT

BRN

RED

39 T

36

FUSE 3A

CONTROL CIRCUITS

DRAWN	SIZE **A**	FSCM NO.	CONTROL WIRING	REV.
ISSUED	SCALE		51	

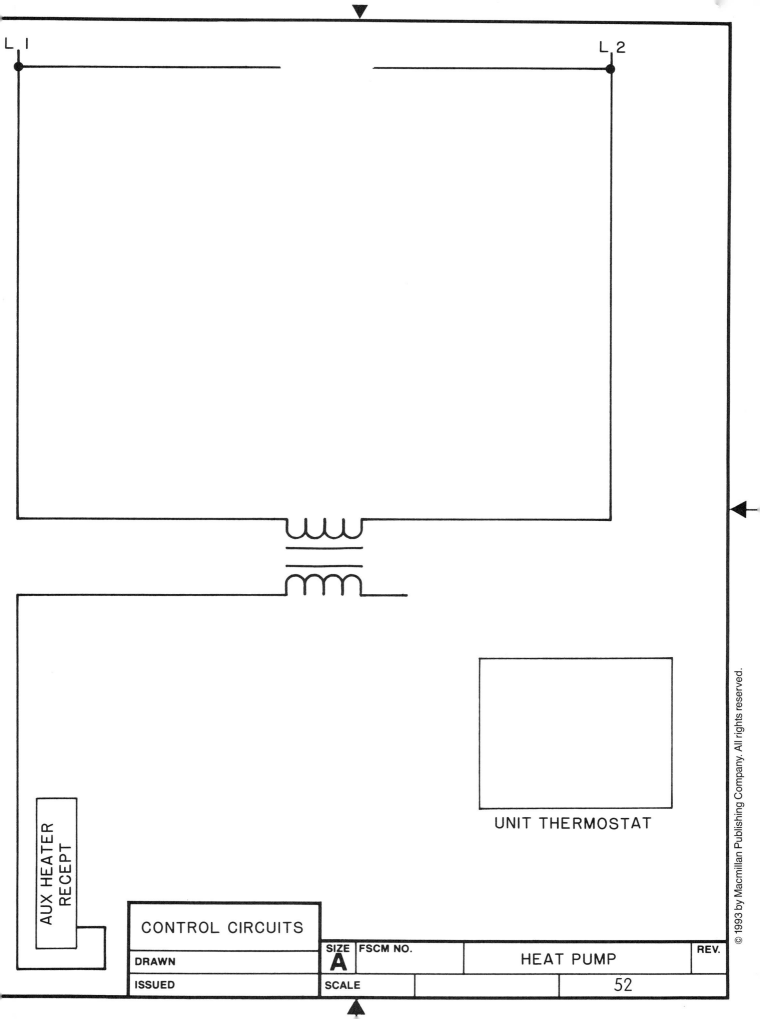

L1

L2

AUX HEATER
RECEPT

UNIT THERMOSTAT

CONTROL CIRCUITS

DRAWN

ISSUED

SIZE
A

FSCM NO.

SCALE

HEAT PUMP

REV.

52

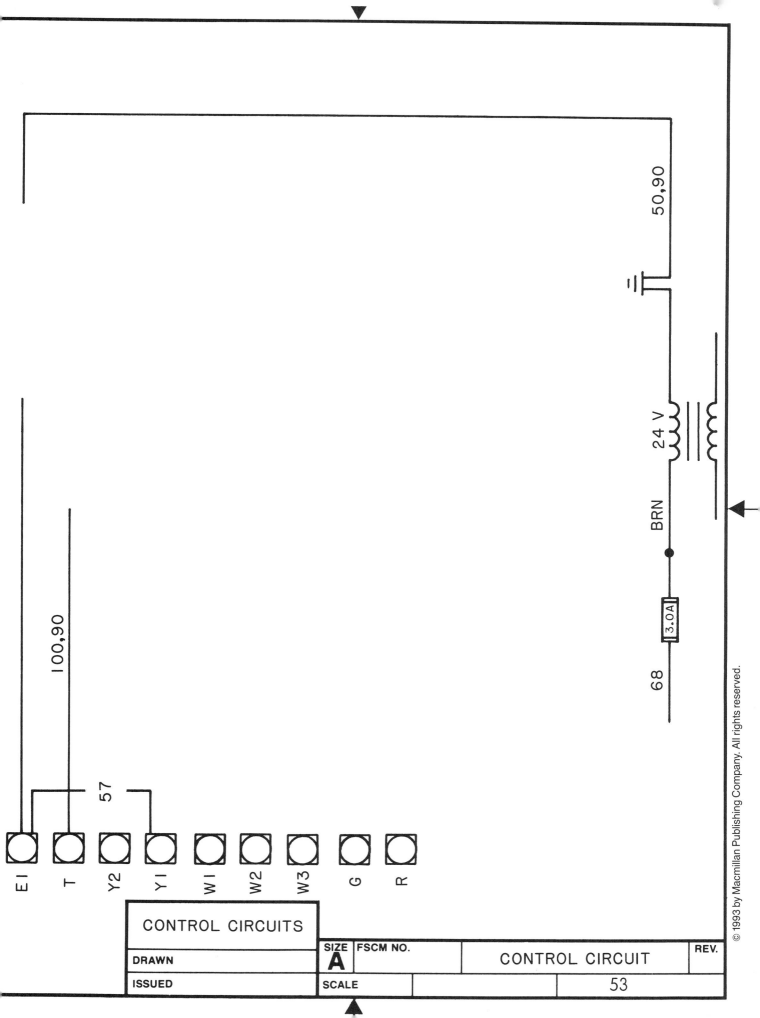

CONTROL CIRCUITS

	SIZE	FSCM NO.		REV.
DRAWN	**A**		CONTROL CIRCUIT	
ISSUED	SCALE		53	

E I

T

Y2

Y I

W I

W2

W3

G

R

100,90

57

50,90

24 V

BRN

3.0A

68

DRAWN	SIZE **A**	FSCM NO.		REV.
ISSUED	SCALE		54	

0° 24

		W ⟶			
	SIZE	FSCM NO.			REV.
DRAWN	A				
ISSUED	SCALE			55	

24

PHASE ANGLE, DEG

| DRAWN | SIZE **A** | FSCM NO. | | REV. |
| ISSUED | SCALE | | SHEET | 56 |

ARM

DRAWN	SIZE **A**	FSCM NO.		REV.
ISSUED	SCALE		SHEET	57

Kin

DRAWN	SIZE	FSCM NO.		REV.
	A			
ISSUED	SCALE		SHEET	58

A

B

DRAWN

ISSUED

SIZE
A

FSCM NO.

SCALE

REV.

SHEET 59

MOTOR

DRAWN	**SIZE** **A**	**FSCM NO.**	**REV.**
ISSUED	**SCALE**		**SHEET** 60

	SIZE	FSCM NO.			REV.
DRAWN	**A**				
ISSUED	SCALE			SHEET	61

GROUND

DRAWN	SIZE **A**	FSCM NO.		REV.
ISSUED	SCALE		SHEET	62

ARMATURE

	SIZE **A**	FSCM NO.		REV.
DRAWN				
ISSUED	**SCALE**		**SHEET** 63	

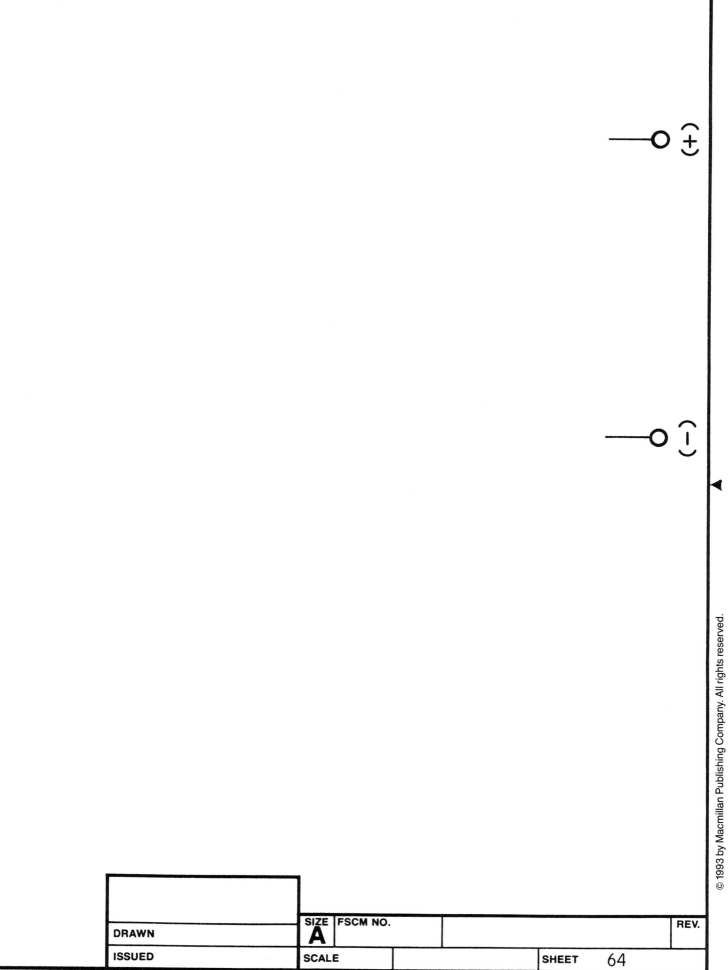

| DRAWN | SIZE **A** | FSCM NO. | | REV. |
| ISSUED | SCALE | | SHEET | 64 |

	SIZE **A**	FSCM NO.		REV.
DRAWN				
ISSUED	SCALE		SHEET 65	

D-C MOTOR, ELECTRIC

DRAWN	SIZE A	FSCM NO.		REV.
ISSUED	SCALE		SHEET	66

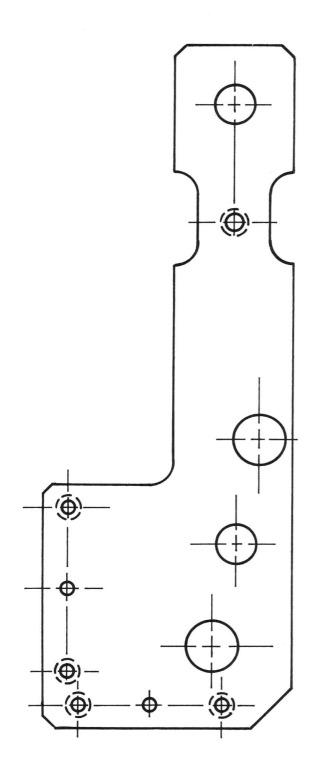

ELECTRONIC PACKAGING					
DRAWN	SIZE **A**	FSCM NO.		CONNECTOR	REV.
ISSUED	SCALE			67	

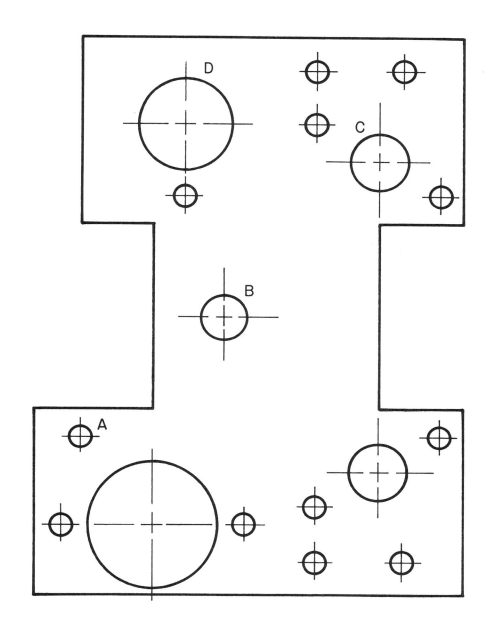

ELECTRONIC PACKAGING				
DRAWN	SIZE **A**	FSCM NO.	PANEL	REV.
ISSUED	SCALE		68	

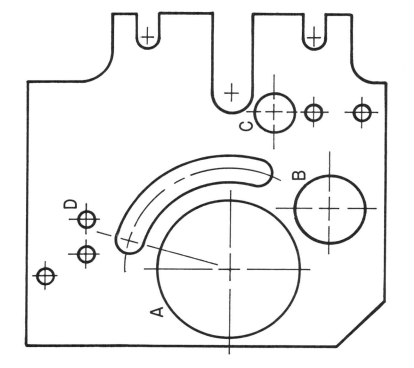

ELECTRONIC PACKAGING				
DRAWN	SIZE **A**	FSCM NO.	POLARIZER BRACKET	REV.
ISSUED	SCALE		69	

ELECTRONIC PACKAGING				
DRAWN	**SIZE** **A**	**FSCM NO.**	HOLD DOWN	**REV.**
ISSUED	**SCALE**		70	

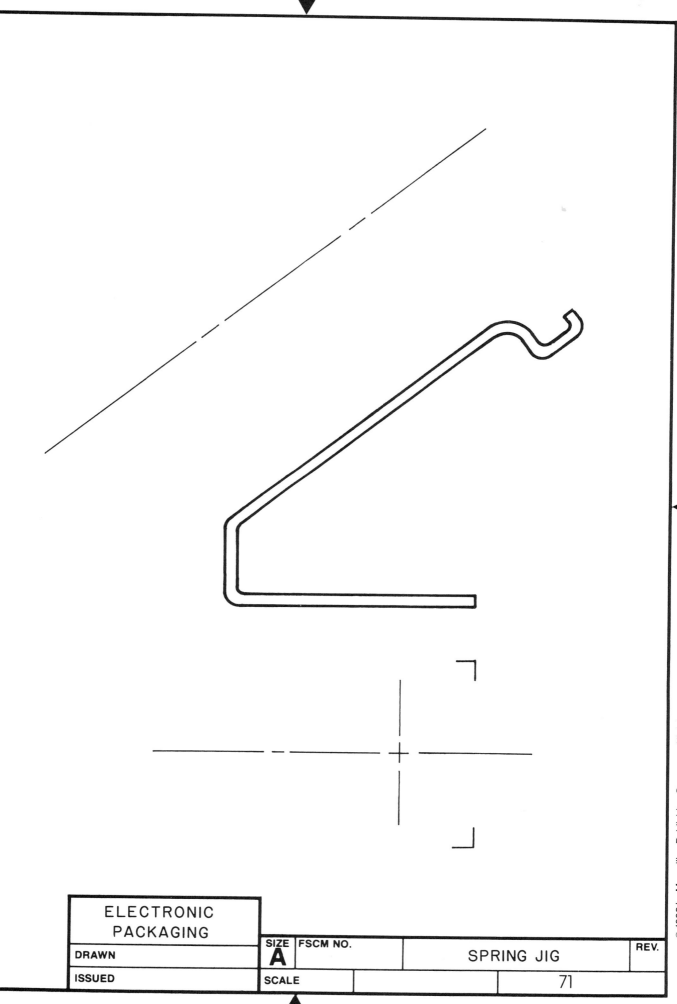

ELECTRONIC PACKAGING					
DRAWN	SIZE **A**	FSCM NO.		SPRING JIG	REV.
ISSUED	SCALE			71	

ELECTRONIC PACKAGING					
DRAWN	SIZE **A**	FSCM NO.		CRT HOLDER	REV.
ISSUED	SCALE			72	

REDUCE TO 2.50 ±.005

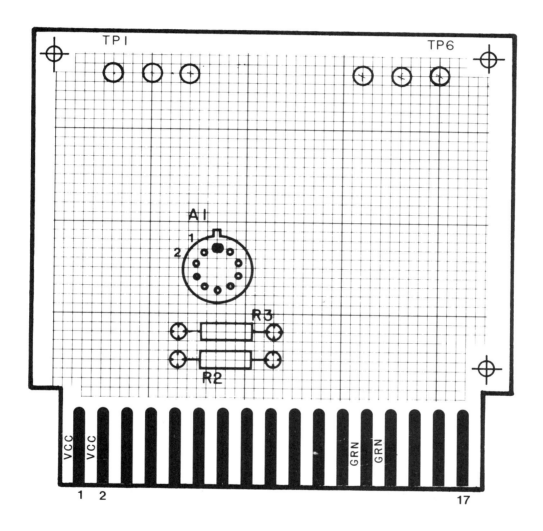

TP1

TP6

A1

1

2

R3

R2

VCC

VCC

GRN

GRN

1 2

17

PCB				
DRAWN	**SIZE** **A**	**FSCM NO.**	ANALOG COMPARATOR	**REV.**
ISSUED	**SCALE** 2/1		73	

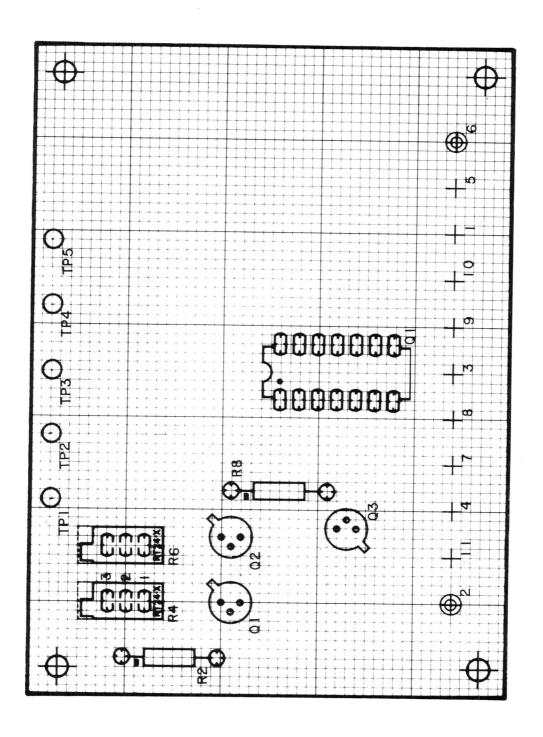

PCB				
DRAWN	**SIZE** **A**	**FSCM NO.**	SCHMITT TRIGGERS	**REV.**
ISSUED	**SCALE** 2/1		74	

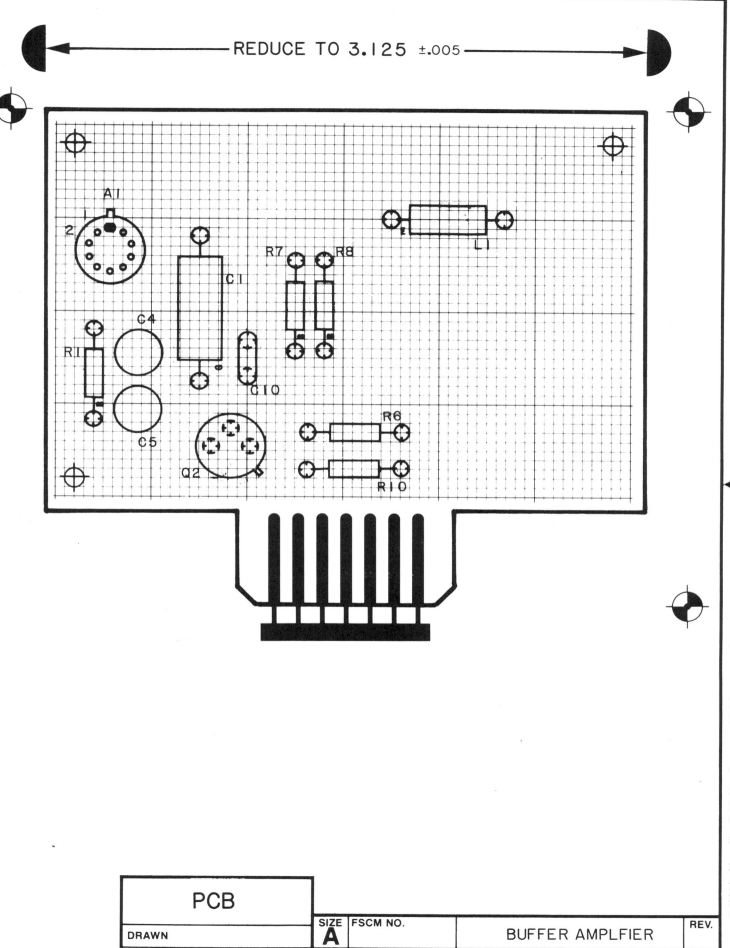

REDUCE TO 3.125 ±.005

PCB				REV.
DRAWN	SIZE **A**	FSCM NO.	BUFFER AMPLFIER	
ISSUED	SCALE 2/1		75	

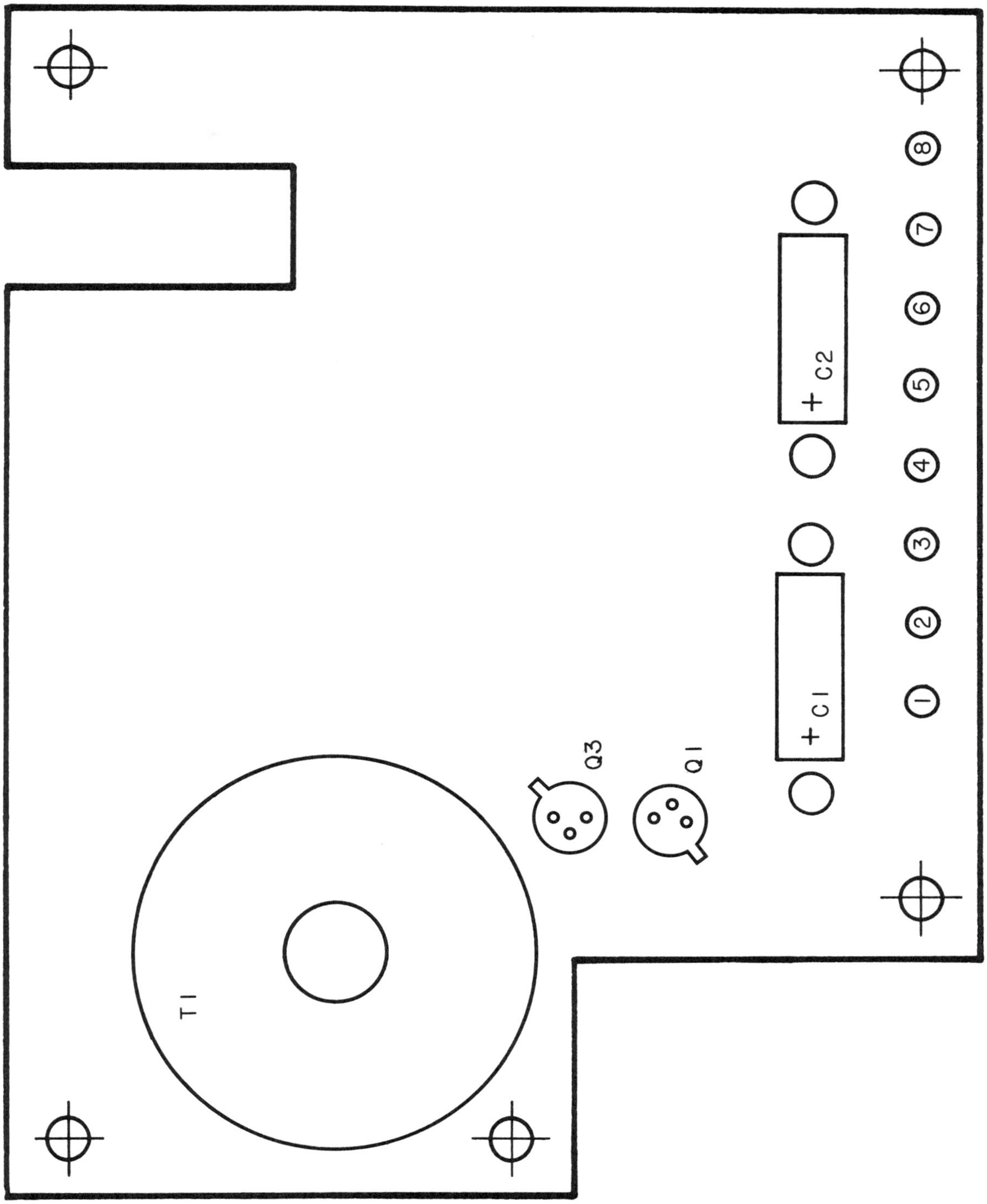

PCB

DRAWN

ISSUED

SIZE	FSCM NO.		2KV NEG POWER SUPPLY	REV.
A				
SCALE 2/1			76	

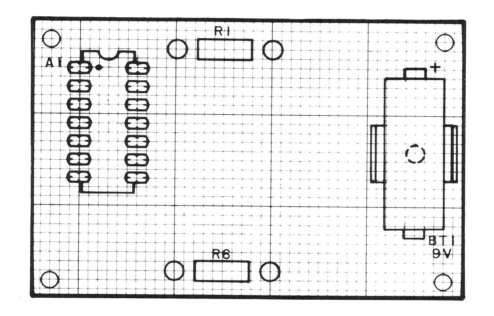

PCB			
DRAWN	SIZE **A** FSCM NO.	FLASHER CIRCUIT	REV.
ISSUED	SCALE 2/1		77

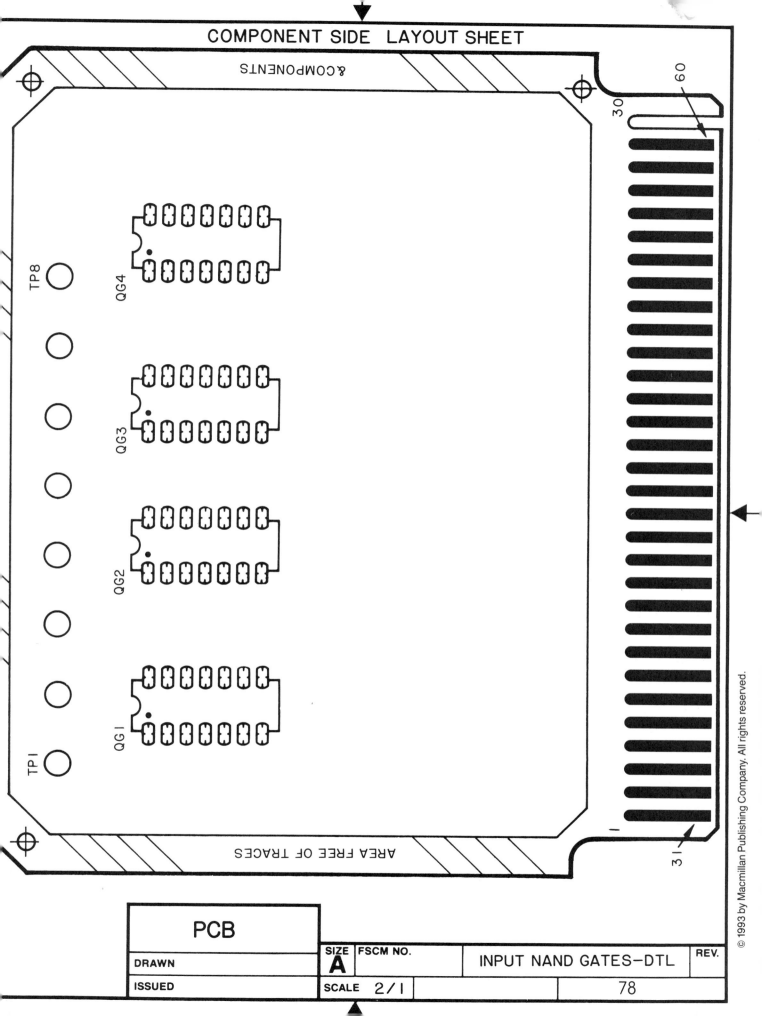

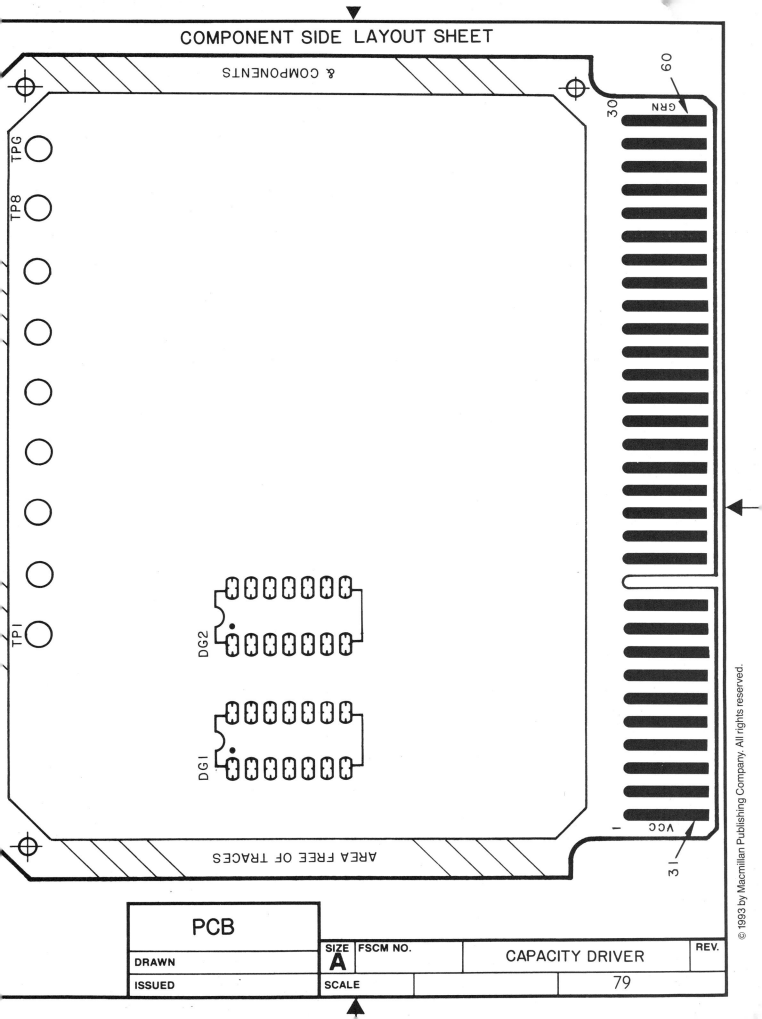

COMPONENT SIDE LAYOUT SHEET

& COMPONENTS

AREA FREE OF TRACES

TPG
TP8
TPI

DG2
DGI

30
60
GRN

VCC
31

PCB

DRAWN

ISSUED

SIZE
A

FSCM NO.

SCALE

CAPACITY DRIVER

REV.

79

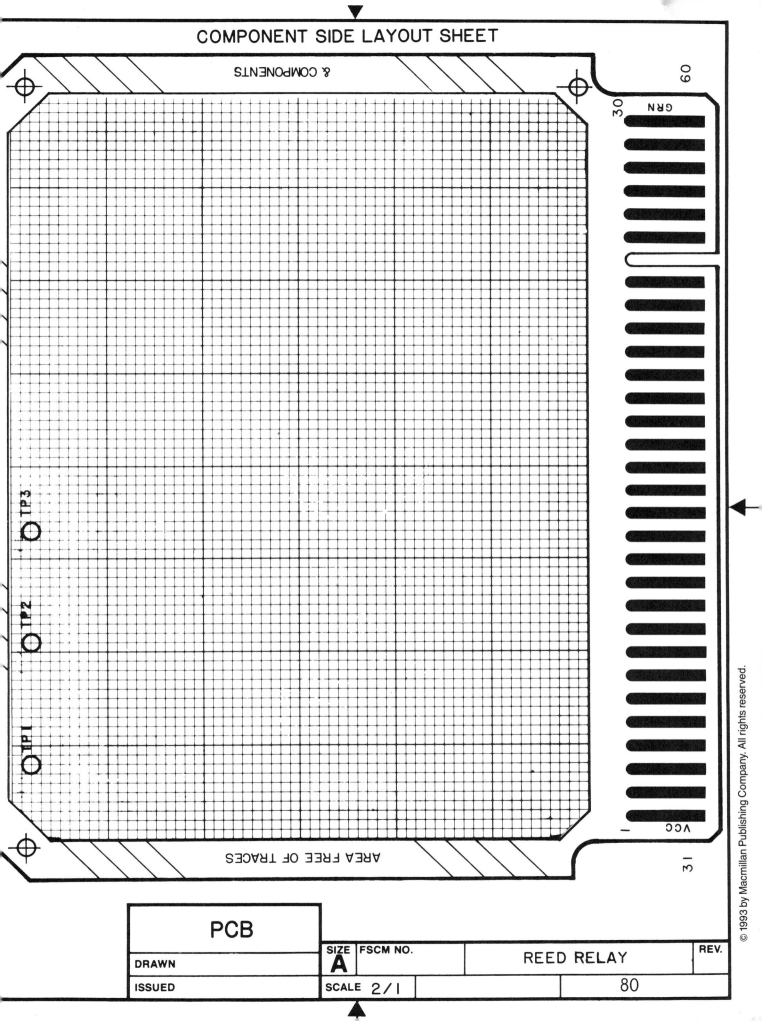

COMPONENT SIDE LAYOUT SHEET

& COMPONENTS

GRN

TP3

TP2

TP1

AREA FREE OF TRACES

VCC

30

60

31

VCC

PCB					
DRAWN	**SIZE** **A**	**FSCM NO.**		**REED RELAY**	**REV.**
ISSUED	**SCALE** 2/1			80	

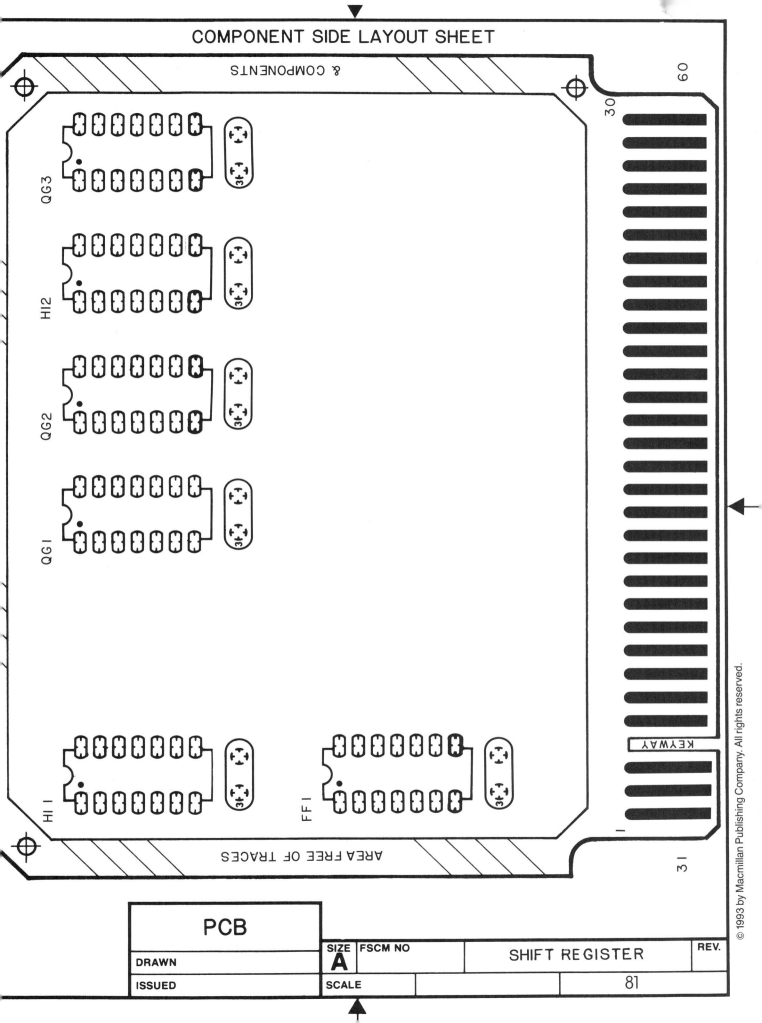

COMPONENT SIDE LAYOUT SHEET

& COMPONENTS

QG3

HI2

QG2

QG1

HI 1

FF1

AREA FREE OF TRACES

30

60

KEYWAY

31

PCB				REV.
DRAWN	SIZE **A**	FSCM NO	SHIFT REGISTER	
ISSUED	SCALE		81	

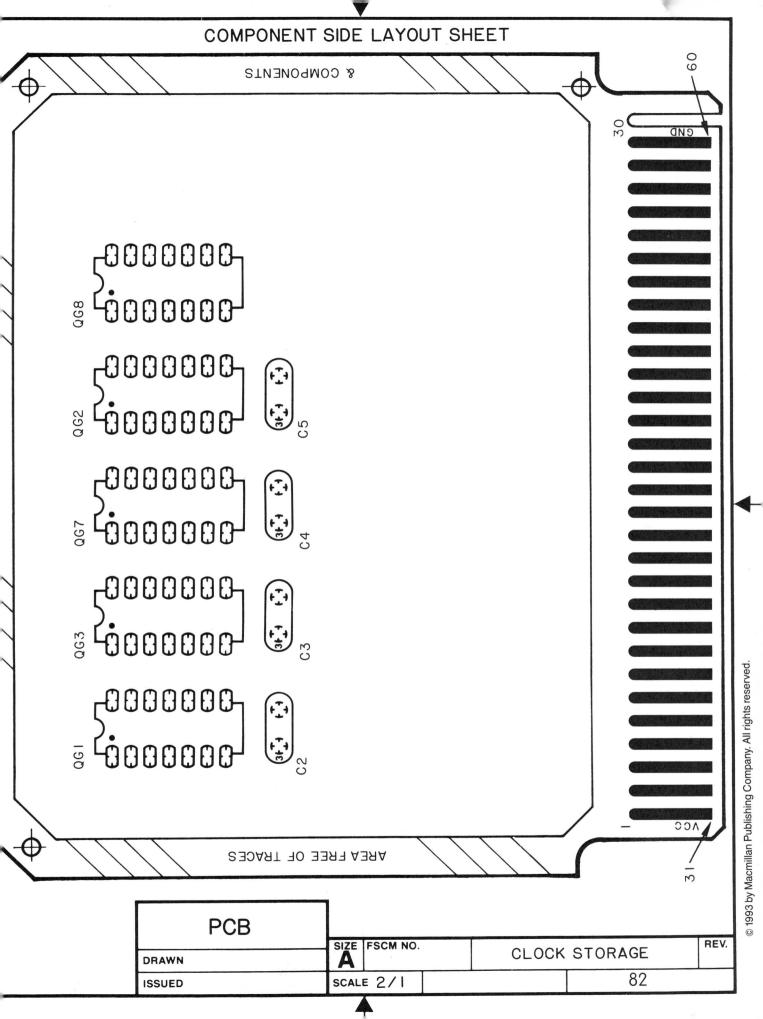

COMPONENT SIDE LAYOUT SHEET

& COMPONENTS

QG8

QG2   C5

QG7   C4

QG3   C3

QG1   C2

AREA FREE OF TRACES

30   60   GND

VCC   31

PCB				
DRAWN	SIZE **A**	FSCM NO.	CLOCK STORAGE	REV.
ISSUED	SCALE 2/1		82	

PARTS
LIST

CHECK BY _____
ENGINEER APV _____

ITEM	REF DESIGNATION OR SPECIFICATION	QTY	MFG NO.	DESCRIPTION	PART NO.

PARTS

LIST

CHECK BY

ENGINEER APV

ITEM	REF DESIGNATION OR SPECIFICATION	QTY	MFG NO.	DESCRIPTION	PART NO.

PARTS
LIST

ITEM	REF DESIGNATION OR SPECIFICATION	QTY	MFG NO.	DESCRIPTION	PART NO.

REV

CHECK BY

ENGINEER APV

PARTS

LIST

REV

CHECK BY _____

ENGINEER APV _____

ITEM	REF DESIGNATION OR SPECIFICATION	QTY	MFG NO.	DESCRIPTION	PART NO.

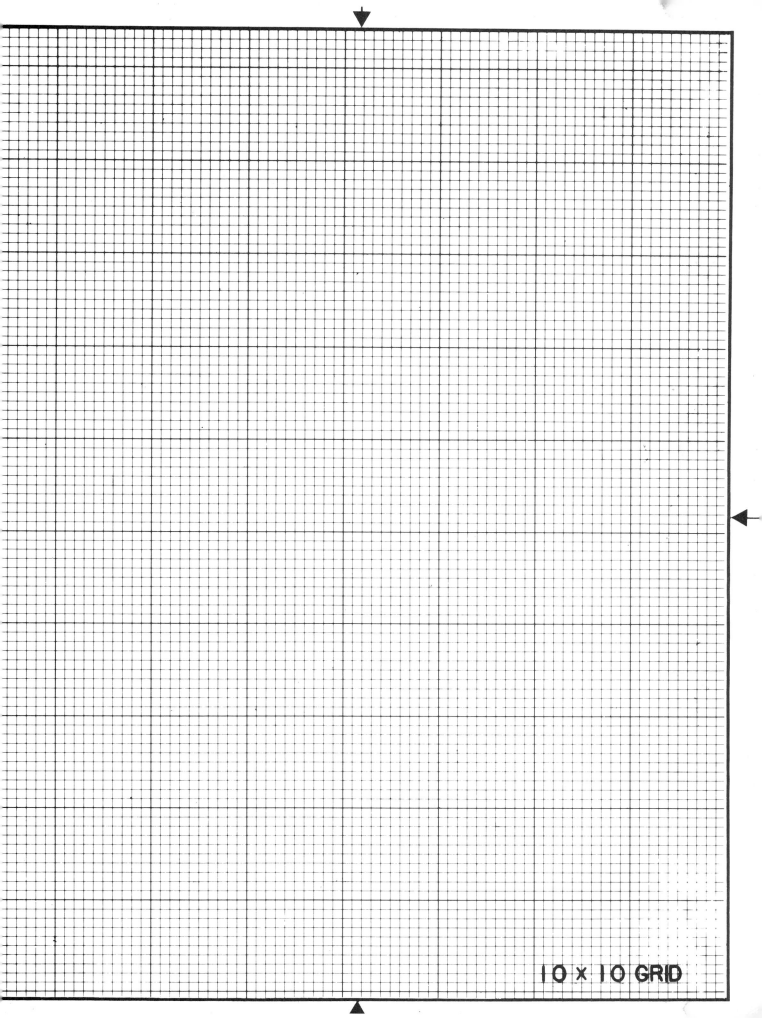

10 × 10 GRID